AF222961

Rewrite for Readability
An Artist's Journey through Generative AI in 2023

Dr. Tristan Behrens

REWRITE FOR READABILITY

An Artist's Journey through Generative AI in 2023

Bibliografische Information der Deutschen Nationalbibliothek: Die Deutsche Nationalbibliothek verzeichnet diese Publikation in der Deutschen National-bibliografie; detaillierte bibliografische Daten sind im Internet über dnb.dnb.de abrufbar.

© 2024 Dr. Tristan Behrens

Herstellung und Verlag: BoD – Books on Demand, Norderstedt

ISBN: 9783758382710

Table of Contents

1. Introduction

An AI-augmented self-portrait of myself. I ran a photograph of me through Midjourney using a process called 'image prompting'. This made me a little younger.

As the year 2023 comes to a close, I ponder upon a new venture: writing my first book. This book would inevitably involve a glimpse into my own life, something I am yet to share on a public platform. To set the foundation for this endeavor, I'll begin with a brief introduction about myself stirred by an exchange of questions and answers I had with an AI offline.

I was born and raised in a quaint village, nestled near the Harz Mountains in Germany, during the colorful era of the 1980s. That was a time when He-Man and the Masters of the Universe captured the imagination of every boy, and Barbie dolls were the desire of every girl. AC/DC's music wafted through our lives and shaped a part of our adolescence. In such invigorating times, nature flourished in close proximity, inspiring a quiet, introverted, and perpetually curious child in me—an eager artist constantly plotting fantastic beasts on paper. The acquisition of our first computer, an IBM compatible with a vulnerable 20 megabyte hard drive, at the beginning of the 1990s, was the fuel to my simmering interests in technology and gaming. Fueled by games like Block Out and Prince of Persia, and Doom and Quake a few years after that, my aspiration to become a game engineer was born.

Reflecting upon my life's journey, it's evident that the people and experiences around me were significant players. My uncle Reiner, a musician, and an electronics engineer, has been instrumental in nurturing my affinity for technology. I owe my early rendezvous with programming to him, including my first ever programming books. Further, I had an enriching encounter with Berlin during a school trip in 1996 when I chanced upon "3D Programmierung mit C++", a book on implementing your own flight simulator.

My life witnessed a pivotal change when I decided to pursue computer science. In a surprising turn of events, I found myself meandering towards music composition and production, stemming from a growing boredom with programming during my studies. This decision to diversify my interests introduced me to the world of music, and significantly changed me.

I embarked upon my professional journey with the belief that a diploma in computer science would guarantee a successful career in programming in Germany. My university, the Clausthal University of Technology, offered excellent courses in discrete mathematics and Artificial Intelligence, sparking my interest. However, the shift in faculty midway through my course presented exciting new prospects with an enhanced focus on Artificial Intelligence.

Describing my personal life, I am proud to hail from a typical German nuclear family with a younger sister. My interests span over a vast spectrum, but if I am to encapsulate them, it is creativity that underlies all my endeavors. Be it visual arts, music, the psychology of creativity, or the socio-economic aspects—it is the creative angle that fascinates me.

On the professional front, I consider my doctoral degree in Computer Science, particularly in Artificial Intelligence, to be a commendable achievement. Equally satisfying is that I have published my own creative music, which was enriched by computational creativity.

Passion is a driving force in my life. It fuels my desire to impart knowledge to others, fervently believing in the potential of learning and creativity as a way to propel people towards abundant productivity. This resonates with my belief that often, a small nudge in the right direction is all that it takes for an individual to unlock unimagined potential. As I embark on this journey through the pages, I hope to encapsulate these experiences and beliefs, offering readers a glimpse into my world and hopefully, a nudge in the right direction.

A robot singing on stage. This picture symbolizes one of the driving forces behind my work: Augmenting human musical creativity with Artificial Intelligence.

I penned this tome driven by twin impulses. Firstly, to capture the whirlwind that was 2023—a year when many, myself included, felt a surge in creative and productive fervor. My stint as the AI Music Artist in Residence at KI Salon Heilbronn bore abundant fruit, while my involvement with the cybernetic electronic heavy metal ensemble Hexagon Machine fueled a relentless stream of inspiration.

Secondly, I've been on an unceasing quest to enhance my work through Artificial Intelligence. AI has seamlessly integrated into my programming, music production, visual arts, and even my writing undertakings. But embarking on the creation of a book, even one as succinct as this, seemed like a worthy challenge to undertake.

Make no mistake—this is not a book written by AI; it is a collaborative dance of human and machine. My thoughts interweave with AI's contributions, both of us editing and refining the narrative. The AI has lent this book its vibrant, poetic prose—a style I've come to cherish and embrace. It's this synergy that inspired the book's title, "Rewrite for Readability."

Within these pages lies a tapestry of chapters, each a fragment of my extensive odyssey with AI. Interspersed are AI-generated images, complete with the prompts that brought them to life, to spark your own imagination. Thank you for your curiosity in my exploits. May the account of my modest ventures serve as a beacon of inspiration for your own path.

1.1. Costs of this book.

In crafting this book, I've opted to bypass the tally of my personal hours invested, choosing instead to spotlight the intriguing expenditure on Artificial Intelligence assistance. The visuals were remarkably cost-free. My in-house AI station's energy usage, a negligible detail, hasn't been factored into the equation. Financially, the narrative shaped by AI was underpinned by a modest $20 investment in a ChatGPT+ subscription. Additionally, the OpenAI API, a frequent tool in my arsenal, added a slight $2.50 to the total. Thus, the AI's contribution to this literary adventure amounted to a mere maximum of $25 (some costs might be unaccounted for)—an economical feat, translating to approximately €22.61 as of December 30th, 2023.

1.2. Disclaimer.

This book is an exploration of Artificial Intelligence (AI) and creativity, incorporating insights from my personal experiences and augmented by AI technologies. While every effort has been made to ensure the accuracy and reliability of the information provided, the nature of AI-generated content means that it can sometimes be imperfect or subject to interpretation. Consequently, I, as the author, do not assume responsibility for any errors, inaccuracies, or misunderstandings that may arise from the content of this book. The material within is provided for informational and entertainment purposes and should not be considered as professional advice. Readers are encouraged to use their discretion and judgment while engaging with the content of this book.

1.3. Prompts

Singing robot:
- Prompt: a terminator robot singing into the microphone on stage pyrotechnics.
- Model: Midjourney V5.

2. AI Art—Computational Creativity—Generative Deep Learning

Embark on a spellbinding journey where imagination meets the transformative power of technology. Welcome to the realm of AI art—a space where creativity pairs with the digital wizardry of computers to craft a new frontier of aesthetic exploration.

Picture a world where machine learning, deep learning, and computer vision converge to conjure up masterpieces. AI art isn't just about creating visuals; it's a dance between technology and the human touch, where algorithms learn to emulate artistic styles, breathe life into novel concepts, or even collaborate with human artists, expanding the horizons of what we dare to dream.

Venture deeper, and you'll discover the enigmatic domain of computational creativity. Here, algorithms don't just follow instructions; they become muses, inventors, and creators. They conjure new ideas, tackle complex problems, and forge works with true value and originality. It's a quest to decode and replicate the elixir of human imagination through the power of computation, showcasing a future where computers don't just compute—they create.

At the heart of this magic lies generative deep learning. Imagine training neural networks—digital brains—to generate content as effortlessly as a painter strokes a canvas. With sophisticated architectures like GANs, VAEs, and Transformers at their core, these networks absorb the essence of existing data and then, like alchemists, transform it into something new and extraordinary. From painting pictures with pixels to weaving tales with words and composing symphonies of sound, these systems redefine the creative landscape.

Take a leap into the captivating realm of Computer Music, where innovation meets the harmonious fusion of technology and artistic expression. This chapter will guide you through the enchanting history of a distinctive form of human creativity, showcasing the incredible possibilities that modern creatives explore on their everyday journeys.

2.1. Mozart's Musical Dice Game

Mozart's musical dice game as imagined by Generative AI. Close to the truth, but a few details are missing.

Wolfgang Amadeus Mozart, the musical genius born in the heart of Salzburg in 1756, is a towering figure whose melodies continue to echo through time. A wunderkind like no other, Mozart was already conjuring up compositions at the age of five and dazzling the courts of Europe with his virtuosity. His oeuvre—a tapestry of over 600 works—encompasses the most cherished symphonies, operas, concertos, and chamber pieces that have come to define the classical canon. Masterworks such as "The Magic Flute," "Don Giovanni," and "The Marriage of Figaro" are testament to his extraordinary melodic instinct, his profound grasp of the human heart, and his unique ability to marry complexity with sheer beauty. Mozart's life, a mosaic of triumphant highs and profound lows, was cut tragically short at 35, leaving behind a legacy that has never ceased to astonish and move us.

Among Mozart's lesser-known but no less intriguing creations is his "Musikalisches Würfelspiel," or musical dice game—a curious union of music and the roll of fate. Published in 1787 and commonly associated with Mozart, this game allows anyone to craft melodies through the serendipitous throw of dice. It stands as one of the most celebrated iterations of such games, which were all the rage in 18th-century Western Europe.

This whimsical game stitches together a composition from a patchwork of 272 musical fragments, guided by a set of rules that hinge on the whims of the dice. Each throw of the dice selects a measure from an array, yielding a unique 16-bar minuet and a 16-bar trio with each play.

Imagine: with a simple toss of two dice and a tally of the pips, you embark on a journey of composition, selecting from Mozart's pre-crafted measures. Sixteen rolls later, a new composition—yours and yet Mozart's—springs to life. Described by the maestro himself, the game was a means to compose German waltzes or Ländler with no musical training—just dice in hand.

Today, the spirit of Mozart's game lives on in the digital realm. Online versions invite you to click and generate a Mozartian piece in an instant, mirroring the simplicity and joy Mozart envisioned. These early attempts at algorithmic composition, where randomness and rules converge to create art, foreshadow the modern world of computer-aided music creation.

Mozart's musical dice game is more than a novelty; it's a window into the playful mind of a luminary, a historical glimpse at the intersection of chance and creativity. To experience this blend of structure and surprise for yourself, you can find it online. Here lies a chance to engage with the past, to let Mozart's genius guide your hand, and to create a piece of music that is uniquely yours, yet touched by the hand of a master.

2.2. A Brief History of Computer Music

Alan Turing who is known for his pioneering work in computing and artificial intelligence also experimented with computer music.

In the evolving narrative of artificial intelligence in music, we trace a journey from the first algorithmic compositions to the sophisticated AI systems of the present day. This evolution reflects not only technological advancements but also the changing relationship between humans and machines in the realm of creativity. Now follows a short overview, which we will unfold a moment later.

1950s: The Genesis of AI in Music

The 1950s marked the embryonic stage of AI in music. It was during this era that early experiments in algorithmic music composition were conducted. Alan Turing, a name synonymous with the foundations of computer science, was a pioneer in this field. His explorations into AI music composition, though not fully appreciated at the time, were groundbreaking.

1960s: The Dawn of Computer Synthesized Sound

As we progressed into the 1960s, the focus shifted to the development of computer programs capable of synthesizing sound. These programs, while rudimentary by today's standards, were instrumental in laying the groundwork for future advancements in AI-generated music.

1970s: Advancements in Music Synthesis

The 1970s witnessed the integration of Digital Signal Processing (DSP) and artificial neural networks into music synthesis. This period was marked by the development of more complex and capable computer programs for music generation, leveraging these new technologies.

1980s: Emergence of Sophisticated AI Music Systems

The 1980s saw the emergence of more sophisticated AI music systems. One notable example from this era is the "Emmy" program, which utilized statistical analysis to generate compositions in the style of classical composers. This period marked a significant step forward in the complexity and diversity of AI-generated music.

1990s: The Role of Machine Learning

The 1990s were characterized by the application of machine learning algorithms in music generation. This allowed computers not only to generate music but also to learn from existing musical compositions, thereby enhancing the quality and complexity of the output.

2000s: The Influence of Deep Learning

In the 2000s, advances in deep learning and neural networks led to the development of even more advanced AI music systems. These systems were capable of generating music that increasingly blurred the line between human and computer-composed music.

2010s: Widespread Application of AI Music Systems

The 2010s saw AI music systems become more widely accessible and used in various applications, including composition, performance, and analysis. The development of platforms like Google's Magenta project illustrated the growing prominence of AI in this creative field.

2020s: Continued Advancements and Diverse Applications

In the current decade, AI music technology continues to evolve, with research focused on developing systems capable of generating more complex and varied music. AI's role in creating music for different media, including video games, films, television, and live performances, is becoming increasingly significant.

This journey of AI in music is a testament to the incredible potential of technology to transform and enrich human creativity. It also highlights the ever-evolving synergy between human and machine in the artistic process. Let us dive deeper into the history of Computer Music.

Many things happened in the 1950s. Rock and roll music is a fine example.

2.2.1 The 1950s

The 1950s, in global popular culture, are remembered as a pivotal era marked by contrasting themes. It was the dawn of rock and roll, with figures like Elvis Presley and Chuck Berry influencing music worldwide. Television began to shape entertainment, introducing iconic shows globally. This decade saw economic prosperity in many parts of the Western world, leading to consumerism and a move towards suburban living. The Cold War, a significant global tension between the USA and the Soviet Union, instilled a sense of political and nuclear apprehension. Internationally, movements for independence and decolonization gained momentum, reshaping political landscapes, especially in Africa and Asia. In fashion, trends varied from the conservative to the rebellious, reflecting the era's diverse cultural shifts.

Also, in the 1950s, the intersection of music and technology witnessed a groundbreaking moment with the creation of the "Illiac Suite," composed by Lejaren Hiller and Leonard Isaacson. This composition, often cited as the first piece of music created by an electronic computer, was crafted using the Illiac I at the University of Illinois.

The "Illiac Suite," initially recognized as String Quartet No. 4, represented a series of four experimental movements. Each movement explored different facets of computer-assisted composition. The first movement focused on generating cantus firmi, reflecting the simplicity yet intricate rules of Renaissance music. The second movement delved into four-voice segments, evolving from random noise to structured music. The third movement, embodying modern 20th-century music, utilized the chromatic scale but required modifications due to its dissonance. The fourth and final movement was the most complex, employing generative grammars and Markov chains to demonstrate the computer's capacity to compose music using non-musical techniques.

The debut of the first three movements in 1956 by a student quartet marked a significant milestone in the fusion of science and art. Hiller's pioneering efforts in this field, however, faced initial resistance from the traditional musical establishment. His work in computational music, which began with the "Illiac Suite," led to the establishment of the Experimental Music Studio (EMS) at the University of Illinois in 1958. This venture further solidified Hiller's position as a key figure in the realm of experimental and computer music.

2.2.2 The 1960s

Amongst other things, people expressed their love for love and peace in the 1960s.

The 1960s were a dynamic and transformative decade globally, characterized by significant social, political, and cultural shifts. It was the era of the Civil Rights Movement in the United States and anti-apartheid movements in South Africa, symbolizing a global push towards racial equality and justice. The decade witnessed the height of the Cold War, including the Cuban Missile Crisis, and the space race, culminating in the 1969 moon landing. Music was revolutionized by the British Invasion, led by bands like The Beatles, and the emergence of rock, folk, and psychedelic genres. The Vietnam War had a profound global impact, sparking widespread anti-war and peace movements. This period also saw the rise of counterculture and youth movements, challenging traditional norms and advocating for freedom of expression, which was reflected in the vibrant and diverse fashion of the era. Additionally, it was a time of significant technological and scientific advancements that reshaped everyday life.

The 1960s marked a significant advancement in the field of computer music, with the development of the first computer programs capable of synthesizing sound. These innovative programs utilized simple algorithms to generate melodies and rhythms, significantly impacting electronic music composition.

John Chowning, a visionary American composer and researcher in computer music, played a pivotal role in this era. He is renowned for developing FM (Frequency Modulation) synthesis. This groundbreaking technique, conceived in the late 1960s, was inspired not by complex mathematical equations but by Chowning's explorations with auditory phenomena and his work in spatialization. His discovery, initially an "ear discovery" rather than a calculated invention, led to the development of commercial synthesizers, such as the Yamaha DX7 in the 1980s.

Max Mathews, an American computer scientist and composer, also made significant contributions during this period. Mathews is credited with creating "Music I," the first computer program for digital sound synthesis, in the late 1950s. His work, which continued to evolve through several iterations of the program, was foundational to the field of computer music and paved the way for future advancements in sound synthesis.

The 1960s thus represented a transformative period in music-making, as these early sound synthesis programs enabled composers to create electronic music using computers. The innovative work of Chowning and Mathews laid the groundwork for the sophisticated AI music systems that would emerge in later decades.

2.2.3 The 1970s

Disco music really took off in the 1970s.

The 1970s were marked by a rich tapestry of cultural, political, and social changes worldwide. This decade saw the continuation and aftermath of the Vietnam War, influencing global attitudes towards peace and military intervention. It was a period of significant economic challenges, including the oil crisis and inflation, impacting economies worldwide. In music, the 1970s were defined by the rise of diverse genres such as disco, punk, and the beginnings of hip-hop, alongside the enduring popularity of rock music with bands like Led Zeppelin and Pink Floyd. The decade was also notable for advancements in environmental awareness and the women's liberation movement, fostering discussions on gender equality and ecological responsibility. Politically, the Cold War continued to influence international relations, while many countries in Africa and Asia navigated post-colonial transitions. In fashion, the 70s were known for their distinctive styles, including bell-bottoms, platform shoes, and vibrant patterns, reflecting the era's spirit of experimentation and self-expression.

The 1970s marked a significant era in the integration of AI with music, characterized by pioneering efforts in computer programs and algorithms for music generation and analysis. This period was instrumental in the development of digital signal processing (DSP) techniques for sound synthesis, enhancing the capabilities of computers in music.

During this decade, innovative computer programs emerged for music generation and analysis. One of the most notable contributions came from Iannis Xenakis, who, although most active in the 1960s, continued to influence the field in the 1970s. Xenakis's work, which combined stochastic processes with music composition, represented a unique blend of mathematics and music, contributing significantly to the development of AI as a supplementary analysis tool in music.

Another remarkable development was the Triadex Muse, created by Edward Fredkin and Marvin Minsky. This device was one of the first digital sequencers and digital logic machines, capable of improvising melodies. The Triadex Muse's innovative approach to algorithmic music production marked a significant advancement in the field, especially considering the technology available at the time.

While the advancements in AI and music during the 1970s were not as sophisticated as later developments like David Cope's Experiments in Musical Intelligence (EMI) in the 1980s, they laid the groundwork for future innovations. The decade saw the emergence of new technologies and methodologies in AI music, marking the beginning of a transformative period in the field. Systems capable of real-time audio signal analysis and the early forays into computer-assisted music composition and analysis set the stage for the more advanced AI music systems that would follow.

2.2.4 The 1980s

Things got serious in the 1980s when counterculture hit its critical mass.

The 1980s were a decade of vivid cultural, political, and technological developments globally. It was characterized by the escalation and eventual conclusion of the Cold War, symbolized by significant events like the fall of the Berlin Wall in 1989. Economically, the era saw the rise of neoliberal policies and a shift towards free-market capitalism, especially in the West. In music, the 1980s were marked by the dominance of pop icons like Michael Jackson and Madonna, the emergence of new wave, and the growth of hip-hop. This decade also witnessed the advent of the digital revolution, with significant advances in computing and the introduction of personal computers. The entertainment industry was transformed by the rise of cable television, video games, and blockbuster movies. Fashion in the 80s was known for its bold colors, shoulder pads, and athletic wear, reflecting a period of extravagance and self-expression. Additionally, the decade saw growing awareness and activism around issues like AIDS and environmental conservation.

The 1980s marked a transformative period in the field of AI and music, characterized by the development of more sophisticated AI music systems. These systems, capable of generating music in various styles, utilized advanced algorithms and techniques, including statistical analysis, to produce new compositions influenced by different musical genres.

A landmark development of this era was the "Emmy" program, created by David Cope, a music professor and composer at the University of California,

Santa Cruz. Emmy leveraged statistical analysis to generate compositions in the style of classical composers like Bach and Mozart. By analyzing extensive data from these composers' works, Emmy learned the statistical patterns and relationships within their music. It then applied this knowledge to create new compositions in similar styles, producing complex and nuanced pieces that were often indistinguishable from human-composed music.

In addition to Emmy, the 1980s witnessed the emergence of other AI music systems employing various approaches, such as rule-based systems and artificial neural networks. These systems were versatile, finding applications in music composition, performance, and analysis, showcasing the expanding capabilities of AI in music.

The advancements in AI music systems during the 1980s represented a significant milestone, enabling computers to generate music that was more intricate and varied than before. The pioneering work of this decade, especially through programs like Emmy, laid the foundation for the advanced AI music systems of future decades, which would incorporate machine learning and deep learning techniques.

2.2.5 The 1990s

The 1990 shifted gears when it came to electronic dance music.

The 1990s were a significant decade globally, marked by profound cultural, technological, and political shifts. It began with the end of the Cold War, leading to a new world order and the emergence of the United States as the sole superpower. This era saw the growth of globalization, with increased economic interdependence and the proliferation of multinational corporations. The technology boom, particularly the rise of the Internet and personal computing, fundamentally transformed communication and information sharing. In music, the 1990s were defined by the popularity of grunge, hip-hop, and boy bands, with iconic artists like Nirvana and Tupac Shakur. The decade was also notable for the rise of environmental consciousness and the discourse on climate change. Fashion trends included the widespread adoption of casual styles like denim, flannel shirts, and sportswear. Politically, the 1990s witnessed significant events like the dissolution of the Soviet Union, the Rwandan Genocide, and the signing of important peace agreements, such as the Oslo Accords in the Middle East. Additionally, the decade saw advancements in science, particularly in genetics, marked by the start of the Human Genome Project.

The 1990s marked a significant era in the field of AI and music, characterized by the introduction and application of machine learning algorithms in music generation. This period saw computers not only creating new compositions but also learning and evolving based on examples of existing music. This advancement allowed for the generation of music that was more complex and varied than ever before.

One of the pivotal advantages of machine learning algorithms in this context was their ability to adapt and improve as they processed more musical data. This adaptability enabled these systems to grasp different musical styles and genres, leading to the creation of music that was increasingly sophisticated and nuanced.

David Cope's "Experiments in Music Intelligence" (EMI) continued in the 1990s. His work in the late 1980s and 1990s with EMI emphasized the concept of recombinancy—combining elements from previous musical works to create new compositions. EMI's approach, focusing on the deconstruction of music into parts and identifying style signatures, laid the foundation for many of the modern AI models in music composition.

During the 1990s, other notable AI music systems were developed, utilizing various techniques including rule-based systems and neural networks. These systems found applications in diverse areas such as music composition, performance, and analysis, showcasing a broadening scope of AI's capabilities in the field of music.

In summary, the 1990s were a crucial decade in AI and music. The integration of machine learning algorithms marked a significant step forward, enabling the creation of more complex and diverse musical compositions. This period set the groundwork for the development of advanced AI music systems in later years, including those employing deep learning techniques.

2.2.6 The 2000s

The first decade of the new millennium showed on so many occasions that mankind grew into a global community because of the internet.

The 2000s marked a pivotal era in the advancement of AI music systems, driven by significant developments in deep learning and neural networks. These technologies enabled AI to analyze and understand music with greater depth, leading to the creation of compositions that closely mirrored human-generated music.

A notable contribution to this field was the 2002 study "Finding Temporal Structure in Music: Blues Improvisation with LSTM Recurrent Networks" by Douglas Eck and Jürgen Schmidhuber. Their research leveraged Long Short-Term Memory (LSTM) networks, a type of recurrent neural network, to analyze and generate blues music. This was a groundbreaking effort in using AI to not only create music but also to understand and replicate the temporal structures and complexities inherent in musical genres.

The 2000s were, a transformative period in AI and music. AI systems developed during this time, like the LSTM networks used by Eck and Schmidhuber, displayed an unprecedented ability to generate music that blurred the lines between compositions crafted by humans and those by machines. The technological advancements in AI music systems during this decade laid the groundwork for further innovations and set the stage for more advanced applications in the music industry. This period was marked by a global context of technological revolution, with the rise of the internet and mobile communications reshaping numerous aspects of society, from social interaction to global politics and economics.

2.2.7 The 2010s

Music became an online streaming phenomenon in the 2010s. Things will never be the same.

Between 2010 and 2019, significant technological advancements occurred globally, marked by the widespread adoption of smartphones and the expansion of social media, which profoundly altered communication and daily life. Developments in artificial intelligence, big data, and cloud computing became pivotal in diverse industries. In the realm of entertainment, the emergence of streaming services revolutionized media consumption, and gaming grew into a major cultural phenomenon. Politically, the decade saw the rise of populist movements across various regions, contributing to increased geopolitical tensions and notable trade disputes among major world economies, reshaping the international political and economic landscape.

In the 2010s, the realm of AI music technology underwent a significant transformation, becoming more accessible and widely utilized across various music-related applications. This era saw an increasing number of artists, musicians, and industry professionals experimenting with AI for music composition, performance, and analysis.

During this decade, the "Melomics" system emerged as a notable example of AI's expanding capabilities in music. Utilizing machine learning algorithms, Melomics was able to generate music in a wide variety of styles. Its ability to create a vast catalog of music without human intervention showcased the increasing sophistication and versatility of AI in the realm of music composition. This system demonstrated a significant leap in AI's ability to not just replicate but also to innovate in music creation, pushing the boundaries of AI's role in the artistic process.

A landmark example of AI's integration into music during this period was the work of Taryn Southern, a singer-songwriter and YouTuber. Southern embraced AI music technology to create her album "I Am AI," released in 2018. Notably, this album was entirely composed and produced using AI, marking a pioneering achievement in the field. She utilized AI music composition software from companies like Amper Music and AIVA, along with technologies from IBM and Google. The creation process involved Southern setting specific musical parameters for the AI and engaging in an iterative process of refining and shaping the music to align with her artistic vision. This approach demonstrated a collaborative synergy between human creativity and AI's capabilities.

Beyond individual artists, companies such as Jukedeck played a crucial role in popularizing AI music technology. Jukedeck offered a platform that allowed users to generate original music based on selected parameters like genre, tempo, and instrumentation. This technology opened new possibilities for creating custom music for diverse applications, including film and television soundtracks, advertising jingles, and video game scores.

Overall, the 2010s marked a period of significant advancement in the field of AI and music. Artists and companies alike leveraged these technologies to produce innovative and original compositions, signifying a notable evolution in the ways music is created and experienced.

2.2.8 The 2020s

The 2020s will be marked in the history books as the decade where Generative AI hit the mainstream.

In the 2020s, AI music technology has been marked by significant advancements and complex challenges. One of the most notable developments is the use of deepfakes in music, which uses AI to synthesize media and can replicate the unique styles and idiosyncrasies of artists. This technology raises serious ethical, moral, and legal questions, especially when AI-generated vocals become indistinguishable from real ones. Holly Herndon's engagement with AI, creating projects that recreate her voice, exemplifies the potential and challenges of this technology.

Several key developments mark this era. In April 2020, the Jukebox model was introduced, generating music with singing in the raw audio domain using a multi-scale VQ-VAE and autoregressive Transformers. By August 2020, the Multi-Track Music Machine (MMM), based on the Transformer architecture, was capable of generating multi-track music with greater user control.

Further advancements came in November 2021 with the introduction of RAVE, a Realtime Audio Variational autoEncoder, enabling fast and high-quality audio waveform synthesis. By September 2022, the AudioLM framework was developed for high-quality audio generation with long-term consistency, extending its application beyond speech to music generation.

The year 2023 saw two significant contributions: Moûsai, which used text-conditional music generation with long-context latent diffusion, and MusicLM, generating high-fidelity music from text descriptions.

Criticism of AI-generated music often revolves around its potential lack of emotional depth and authenticity compared to human compositions. For instance, AI renditions attempting to mimic the style of famous artists have been criticized for not fully capturing the original's essence. The music industry's response to AI in music is mixed, with some musicians appreciating its utility in production, while others raise concerns about its impact on creativity and job security.

Additionally, the integration of AI in music creation introduces complex copyright and intellectual property issues. Some platforms allow users to claim copyright ownership of AI-generated compositions, but the legal framework is still evolving. The music industry must navigate these legal complexities while exploring AI's creative possibilities.

2.3. References

- Musikalisches Würfelspiel: https://dice.humdrum.org/
- Analytics Vidhya. "*Exploring the World of Music Generation with AI.*" https://www.analyticsvidhya.com/blog/2023/07/exploring-the-world-of-music-generation-with-ai/
- Thomann. "*The Rise of Artificial Intelligence in Music – No worries?*" https://www.thomann.de/blog/en/the-rise-of-ai-in-music-2/
- Wikipedia. "*Music and artificial intelligence.*" https://en.wikipedia.org/wiki/Music_and_artificial_intelligence
- Wikipedia. "*Illiac Suite.*" https://en.wikipedia.org/wiki/Illiac_Suite
- Illinois Distributed Museum. "*ILLIAC and ORDVAC*" https://distributedmuseum.illinois.edu/exhibit/illiac_and_ordvac/
- Britannica. "*Illiac Suite for String Quartet.*" https://www.britannica.com/topic/Illiac-Suite-for-String-Quartet
- Wikipedia. "*Lejaren Hiller.*" https://en.wikipedia.org/wiki/Lejaren_Hiller
- Yamaha Hub. "*Discovering Digital FM: John Chowning Remembers.*" https://hub.yamaha.com/discovering-digital-fm-john-chowning-remembers/
- Wikipedia. "*John Chowning.*" https://en.wikipedia.org/wiki/John_Chowning
- Wikipedia. "*Frequency Modulation Synthesis.*" https://en.wikipedia.org/wiki/Frequency_modulation_synthesis

- Sound On Sound. *"John Chowning."* https://www.soundonsound.com/people/john-chowning
- Watt AI. *"The Evolution of Music and AI Technology."* https://watt-ai.github.io/blog/music_ai_evolution
- Computer History Museum. *"Algorithmic Music – David Cope and EMI."* https://computerhistory.org/blog/algorithmic-music-david-cope-and-emi/
- JSTOR. *"Composing with Algorithms: An Interview with David Cope."* https://www.jstor.org/stable/40072590](https://www.jstor.org stable/40072590
- Wikipedia. *"David Cope."* https://en.wikipedia.org/wiki/David_Cope
- LiveInnovation.org. *"David Cope: A Lifetime Contribution to Artificial Intelligence and Music."* https://liveinnovation.org/david-cope-a-lifetime-contribution-to-artificial-intelligence-and-music/
- Band Pioneer. *"Using AI to Create Music of the Future."* https://bandpioneer.com/reviews/exploring-the-new-frontier-of-ai-music-generators
- Wikipedia. *"Taryn Southern."* https://en.wikipedia.org/wiki/Taryn_Southern
- DJMag.com. *"AI Futures - how artificial intelligence will change music."* https://djmag.com/longreads/ai-futures-how-artificial-intelligence-will-change-music
- CelebrityAccess. *"AI In Music Production - Advancements, Collaborations & Copyright Issues."* https://celebrityaccess.com/2023/12/21/ai-in-music-production-advancements-collaborations-copyright-issues/
- OpenAI. *"Jukebox: A Generative Model for Music."* https://arxiv.org/abs/2005.00341
- Pardo, Bruno et al. *"MMM : Exploring Conditional Multi-Track Music Generation with the Transformer."* https://arxiv.org/abs/2008.06048
- Kim, Jaehoon et al. *"RAVE: A variational autoencoder for fast and high-quality neural audio synthesis."* https://arxiv.org/abs/2111.05011
- OpenAI. *"AudioLM: a Language Modeling Approach to Audio Generation."* https://arxiv.org/abs/2209.03143
- OpenAI. *"Moûsai: Text-to-Music Generation with Long-Context Latent Diffusion."* https://arxiv.org/abs/2301.11757
- OpenAI. *"MusicLM: Generating Music From Text."* https://arxiv.org/abs/2301.11325

2.4. Prompts

Musical Dice Game:
- Positive prompt: Wolfgang Amadeus Mozart's musical dice game
- Steps: 20
- Sampler: DPM++ 2M Karras
- CFG scale: 7
- Seed: 792470017
- Size: 1344x768
- Model: albedobaseXL_v13

Alan Turing:
- Positive prompt: alan turing working on computer music. abstract painting.
- Steps: 20
- Sampler: DPM++ 2M Karras
- CFG scale: 7
- Seed: 3803005108
- Size: 1344x768
- albedobaseXL_v13

1950s Rock and Roll Couple Portrait:
- Positive prompt: A portrait of a rock and roll couple from the 1950s
- Negative prompt: Deformed
- Steps: 20
- Sampler: DPM++ 2M Karras
- CFG scale: 7
- Seed: 2813967267
- Size: 1344x768
- Model: albedobaseXL_v13

1960s Woodstock Festival Couple Portrait:
- Positive prompt: A portrait of a couple from the 1960s at the Woodstock festival. Love, peace, and flower power.
- Negative prompt: Deformed
- Steps: 20
- Sampler: DPM++ 2M Karras
- CFG scale: 7
- Seed: 435999300

- Size: 1344x768
- Model: albedobaseXL_v13

1980s Musicians Group Painting:
- Positive prompt: A painting of a small group of four musicians from the 1980s. Subculture, counterculture, underground scene, punks, and goths.
- Steps: 20
- Sampler: DPM++ 2M Karras
- CFG scale: 7
- Seed: 3895616758
- Size: 1344x768
- Model: albedobaseXL_v13

1990s Techno Fans Painting:
- Positive prompt: Painting of techno fans in the 1990s. Ravers, eurodance, nightclub.
- Steps: 20
- Sampler: DPM++ 2M Karras
- CFG scale: 7
- Seed: 4013523652
- Size: 1344x768
- Model: albedobaseXL_v13

Robot-Dressed DJs Painting:
- Positive prompt: A painting of two DJs dressed up as robots.
- Steps: 20
- Sampler: DPM++ 2M Karras
- CFG scale: 7
- Seed: 1940528452
- Size: 1344x768
- Model: albedobaseXL_v13

Avant-Garde Female Pop Star Oil Painting
- Positive prompt: Oil painting of a female pop star or musician with long straight platinum blonde hair with bangs reaching down to her eyebrows. Wearing oversized, futuristic-looking black sunglasses with a reflective surface, and fingerless black gloves.
- Negative prompt: Photograph, round sunglasses, too many fingers

- Steps: 20
- Sampler: DPM++ 2M Karras
- CFG scale: 7
- Seed: 1356258844
- Size: 1344x768
- Model: albedobaseXL_v13

2020 K-Pop Group Painting
- Positive prompt: A painting of a K-pop group in the year 2020.
- Negative prompt: Deformed, photograph
- Steps: 20
- Sampler: DPM++ 2M Karras
- CFG scale: 7
- Seed: 2947235071
- Size: 1344x768
- Model: albedobaseXL_v13

3. The Human Artist in the Center of the Creative Endeavour

Each time I delve into the discussion about my work in Generative AI, an assumption frequently surfaces from the audience. They often believe that the mesmerizing content I exhibit is the result of a mere click of a button, that the AI takes the reins and accomplishes everything autonomously. However, this is far from reality. In truth, Generative AI is merely a cog in the intricate machinery of the process. It necessitates significant human interaction and a rigorous feedback loop. The magic doesn't just happen; it's carefully crafted.

In an era where Generative AI is rapidly seeping into our daily productivity and creativity, the discussion surrounding its influence grows more frequent. Ever since the release of ChatGPT in the Autumn of 2022 and its following widespread acceptance, it's clear that we're on a one-way track—there's no reversing this trend. Hence, it is crucial to articulate my perspective, an outlook that is echoed by many of my professional peers and those beyond my field.

Here's the crux of the matter: there is a stark contrast between music that is solely generated by AI and music that is created in collaboration with AI. This distinction is not limited to music alone, but applies to all content. And I must emphasize that my interest lies heavily in the collaborative aspect—the 'with' part of the equation. To be quite frank, the concept of AI creating content in isolation, without any or very small human input, is rather dull to me. Let us dig deeper...

3.1. Gary Kasparov, Deep Blue and Centaur Freestyle Chess

In the annals of chess and artificial intelligence, the spirited battles between renowned chess grandmaster Gary Kasparov and IBM's supercomputer, Deep Blue, hold a place of prominence.

Their first clash occurred in 1996, with a series of six captivating games. The opening match was a shock to the world, as the reigning world champion, Kasparov, tasted defeat at the hands of a computer in a tournament setting—a first in the history of the game. However, Kasparov demonstrated his resilience and strategic genius, bouncing back to claim a 4-2 victory over Deep Blue. The games were a fascinating display of human strategic depth pitted against pure computational prowess.

Garry Kasparov playing chess with a robot. In my humble opinion, Kasparov is a reason for optimism when it comes to augmenting human potential with Artificial Intelligence.

The chess world waited with bated breath for the 1997 rematch, which attracted global attention, not merely from chess aficionados but also from those intrigued by advancements in artificial intelligence. The tables turned this time, with Deep Blue triumphing over Kasparov 3½-2½. The second game of this match sparked controversy when Kasparov accused IBM of cheating. However, after a detailed analysis, he subsequently withdrew his allegations.

These historic face-offs birthed a new concept in chess—advanced chess or centaur chess. Here, human players employ computer programs to navigate potential moves. The essence of centaur chess lies in the collaboration between human and computer, with the human having the final say. This evolved into freestyle chess, a blend of human strategic prowess and computer analytical superiority. The result is a formidable duo that regularly crafts games bordering on perfection.

Online tournaments for advanced chess or centaur freestyle chess have gained popularity, drawing players of varying skill levels from around the globe. These tournaments typically commence with elimination rounds, culminating in a round-robin finale among the leading players. These finalists, often referred to as "centaurs", embody the perfect blend of human-computer gameplay.

The historical showdowns between Kasparov and Deep Blue, followed by the evolution of advanced and centaur chess, underscore the riveting interplay between human intelligence and artificial intelligence in the world of chess.

For me this is a prime example of the evolution of human machine interaction and collaboration.

The captivating genesis of chess can be traced back as far as the 7th century. The earliest written records about this intriguing game, found in ancient Pahlavi and Sanskrit texts, take us on an exciting journey through time. One such text, the Chatrang-namak, paints a vivid picture of chess as a mesmerizing reenactment of a battlefield. In this portrayal, each chess piece embodies a different military rank or role.

This tale, spun by Bozorgmehr during the reign of the illustrious Khosrow I, suggests that chess, referred to as Chatrang in Pahlavi, journeyed to Persia from the exotic lands of India. The oldest known chess manual we have today, Kitab ash-shatranj, written by al-Adli ar-Rumi, a renowned Arab chess player circa 840, echoes this account of Persian chess's intriguing Indian roots.

While the 20th century witnessed a consensus that chess was born in the enchanting lands of northwest India in the early 7th century, this popular belief has been put under the microscope in more recent times, inviting readers to delve deeper into the mysterious origins of this timeless game.

A picture that is loosely based on the 'Mechanical Turk' idea. A robot that plays chess. Centuries ago it was a fake, today chess computers are a reality.

Imagine a time in 1770 when a machine known as 'The Mechanical Turk,' also referred to as the Automaton Chess Player, was unveiled by its creator, Wolfgang von Kempelen. This chess-playing marvel was more than just a machine; it was an enigma that held audiences spellbound for over eight decades. The Turk was presented as an extraordinary automaton, deftly capable of not only engaging in intense chess matches against human challengers but also of solving the complex knight's tour puzzle.

Yet, beneath its mechanical facade lay a secret so profound, so ingenious, it was nothing short of a masterpiece. The Turk was no automaton; it was a brilliantly orchestrated illusion. Nestled within its intricate design was a human chess maestro, surreptitiously controlling the Turk's every move. This cunning deception allowed the Turk to triumph over some of the era's most notable luminaries, including the likes of Napoleon Bonaparte and Benjamin Franklin.

The Mechanical Turk's true identity, however, remained shrouded in mystery, its secret safeguarded until its untimely demise in a fire in 1854. Only then was its true nature as a grand hoax revealed, leaving the world in astonished disbelief. Throughout the Turk's fascinating journey, it was secretly operated by various chess virtuosos, including Johann Allgaier and William Lewis, who maintained its enigmatic allure and continued its legacy of captivating audiences.

In the world of chess, computers have become a force to be reckoned with. Imagine a machine that not only offers practice and analysis for chess enthusiasts but also serves as an engaging opponent. This is the realm of computer chess, a fascinating blend of hardware and software engineered to play the royal game.

Today, we have chess applications of grandmaster stature available across various platforms. From the might of supercomputers to the convenience of smartphones, these applications are both standalone machines and free open-source software like the highly renowned Stockfish and GNU Chess.

They work by utilizing heuristic methods, a kind of problem-solving strategy that helps them build, search, and evaluate enormous trees of potential move sequences. Harnessing the immense computational power of modern computers, these applications can process thousands to millions of nodes per second.

The journey of computer chess is a remarkable tale of technological evolution. In the 1950s, the first steps were taken with rudimentary programs operating on vacuum-tube computers. In the beginning, these programs were relatively weak. However, like a fledgling chess player honing their skills, they improved dramatically over time.

By 1997, a milestone was reached. Chess engines, working on supercomputers or specialized hardware, could triumph over top human players. Just under a decade later, by 2006, this great feat was made possible even on desktop PCs.

Despite these advancements, the game of chess with its labyrinthine complexity remains an enigma that even the most advanced computers cannot completely solve. Yet, the evolution of computer chess from a pioneering AI challenge to a scientifically completed field has been remarkable. Today, it's seen as a routine computing task, yet it continues to captivate and challenge both human players and AI developers alike.

The narrative of Gary Kasparov's encounter with Deep Blue is a profound revelation of a long-held belief being shattered. For eons, it was considered an exclusive human capability to outwit and outmaneuver in the intricate game of chess. However, after relentless effort spanning decades, and arguably centuries, a revelation was born—a machine capable of thought could indeed defeat a chess grandmaster.

But Kasparov was far from defeated. Instead of surrendering to a future dominated by machines, he chose to harness their power, blending it with his own intellectual prowess. By integrating mathematics and computing into his repertoire, he elevated his own creativity and productivity to new heights.

This tale encapsulates our current journey, as we continue to find ways to augment our own abilities, not with a sense of defeat, but with a spirit of innovation and enhancement. It's a powerful testament to the unending potential of human-machine synergy.

3.2. Replacing the By with a With

In my personal perspective, the crux of what we term as artificial intelligence lies in the collaboration between humans and machines, with particular emphasis on the human aspect. Let's embark on a journey to further explore this fascinating field.

For the purpose of our discussion, let's consider music composition, though I'm quite certain our conclusions will extend to other creative domains as well. Let's differentiate between three types of compositions:

- Music composed purely by humans.
- Music composed solely by computers.
- Music that's a result of a symbiotic relationship between humans and computers.

When we talk about Generative AI in the context of music composition, it's important to distinguish between music composed by AI and music composed with AI. The former is akin to pressing a button and receiving a song, while the latter represents a dynamic, ongoing dialogue between man and machine that ultimately leads to a unique creative artifact. This is of course a repetition of what I have said before. This idea is so important that it needs to by repeated.

My personal focus is music created with AI. I see the human in the center of the creative enterprise, orchestrating a collection of different tools for music production that includes but is not limited to tool that use Artificial Intelligence. It is the human mindset, the background, the situation, the emotions and the goal that drives the creative process. So far machines lack a few of these properties.

The creative octopus is a fine representation of the creative cyborg, a human that has a lot of creative tools at their disposal and is the driving force behind every artistic endeavor.

If you were to step into my realm of music creation, you'd find yourself amidst a flurry of activity akin to a human octopus, each arm engaged in a unique aspect of the creative process.

Picture this: I summon my personally designed Deep Neural Networks, calling upon them to flesh out the skeleton of a melody that is resonating with my current disposition and artistic intentions. I begin by requesting a compelling bassline, bar by bar, utilizing my chosen instruments. An engaging dialogue ensues between the AI and me, as we refine and perfect the bassline to my liking. Sometimes, it's a dance of genres; other times, it's a matter of tweaking the last bar to hit the right chord. Once I am content with the bassline, I request a fitting drum beat with a specified number of drum events.

The foundation is now laid. Next, I request a slick guitar riff to layer over the bass and drums. If I'm feeling particularly adventurous, I might even call for the addition of strings, a piano, or a synthesizer. The beauty of this process is that it's not bound by convention—I can begin anywhere my muse guides me.

With the skeleton of the melody, harmony and rhythm now formed, I turn my attention to structuring the song. This involves crafting an intro, verses, choruses, prechoruses, bridges, and an outro. The intro sets the tone and prepares the listener for the narrative that is about to unfold. The verses, delivering the lyrical content, often feature a repeating melody and chord progression. The chorus, or refrain, is the song's catchy, easily remembered hook, repeated several times. The prechorus serves as a bridge, building anticipation and setting up the chorus, often introducing contrasting melodies or chord progressions. The actual bridge provides a break from the established structure, introducing fresh musical elements. Finally, the outro, a satisfying conclusion that brings the composition to a gratifying end.

Simultaneously, I am also curating the timbre, or the "color" of the sound. This characteristic, determined by the quality and combination of frequencies and overtones, allows us to distinguish between different sounds, even when played at the same volume and note. My AI creates the skeleton, the sheet music, which I then breathe life into by routing the notes through various (electronic) instruments and drum kits.

The next phase is mixing. This process involves combining multiple layers of audio—vocals, instruments, effects—into a final stereo track. It's about adjusting levels, panning, and applying effects like EQ, compression, and reverb to create a cohesive, balanced sound that enhances the overall quality of the song. It's a critical step that shapes how the individual elements merge in the final output.

Lastly, I embark on the journey of mastering. This final step fine-tunes the mixed audio tracks, ensuring they sound their best across all playback systems. It involves equalization, compression, limiting, and stereo enhancement to create a balanced, cohesive sound. Mastering also ensures consistency in sound and volume across an album and prepares the recording for distribution by adding metadata and finalizing the format. This last step polishes the audio, preparing it for public release. For this phase, I do use AI-based tools to augment my work.

This is my creative process, a symphony of technology and human artistry, breathing life into the notes and transforming them into soul-moving music.

In an intriguing aside, the unique processes involved in these and similar workflows arguably elevate the resulting music to a level that warrants copyright protection. In contrast to a purely generative approach, where one merely pushes a button and the AI creates, these methods place the human element firmly at the center. This 'human-in-the-loop' approach ensures a certain level of creative originality or 'Schöpfungshöhe', as it's known in legal parlance. Consequently, music composed with the aid of AI could reasonably be granted copyright protection, while music composed solely by an AI would not.

Get inpired by the above and show that the same picture applies to other creative fields. Write examples for a few creative domains of your choice.

3.3. From Music to other Creative Fields

In the realm of music production, the meeting of artificial intelligence and human ingenuity creates an orchestra of boundless creativity. This symphony isn't confined to the domain of music alone, it echoes across multiple artistic disciplines, birthing masterpieces that are both innovative and soul-stirring. Let's delve into this captivating world where technology and human touch dance in perfect harmony.

Digital Painting and Graphic Design: Picture a digital painter, presented with a sketch, a rough outline by an AI. It's a starting point, a foundation. The artist then weaves in their magic, injecting their unique style into the canvas. They manipulate colors, add elements, and breathe life into the AI's concept. The end result? A piece of art that marries computer precision with human creativity.

AI-assisted Writing: Imagine a storyteller, aided by an AI that cooks up plot twists, character arcs, or even drafts sections of the text. The writer then steps in, the maestro of the narrative, adding layers of emotion, intrigue, and authenticity to the AI-proposed story. The final piece resonates with the reader, a tale spun from the blend of machine intelligence and human imagination.

Film and Video Production: Visualize a director, using AI for initial storyboarding, shot compositions, or creating rudimentary visual effects. Yet, it is the director's touch that refines these raw elements into a cinematic masterpiece. The subtle play of light, the deliberate camera angles, the soulful actor performances—none of this can be replicated by AI. The end product is a beautiful balance of technology and human vision, a film that strikes a chord with its audience.

Architecture and Interior Design: Consider an architect, employing AI to generate structural designs or layouts. The architect then steps in, infusing these designs with aesthetic appeal and functionality, crafting spaces that not only exist but live and breathe. They select materials, colors, and textures that transform the AI-proposed models into spaces that echo with human warmth and comfort.

Culinary Arts: Think of a chef, with an AI suggesting ingredient combinations and recipe structures. But it is the chef's expertise that brings this to life, balancing flavors, adjusting cooking techniques, and presenting a dish that sings a symphony of tastes.

In each of these instances, AI is an invaluable tool, a muse that offers efficiency and novel ideas. Yet, the soul of the creation, the emotional depth, the creative nuances—they all spring from the human touch. This marriage of AI capabilities and human creativity births products that are innovative and deeply personal, similar to the symphony we see in music production.

3.4. References

- Wikipedia. "*Deep Blue versus Garry Kasparov.*"
  https://en.wikipedia.org/wiki/Deep_Blue_versus_Garry_Kasparov
- Chess.com. "*Deep Blue Kasparov Chess.*"
  https://www.chess.com/article/view/deep-blue-kasparov-chess
- Wikipedia. "*Advanced Chess.*"
  https://en.wikipedia.org/wiki/Advanced_Chess

3.5. Prompts

Garry Kasparov:
- Positive prompt: chess grandmaster garry kasparov shaking hands with a robot over a chessboard. magnificent and dramatic lighting. masterpiece photography. cyberpunk futurism. cyber lights. depth of field.
- Negative prompt: deformed

- Steps: 20
- Sampler: DPM++ 2M Karras
- CFG scale: 7
- Seed: 1608911474
- Size: 1344x768
- Model: albedobaseXL_v13

Mechanical Turk:
- Positive prompt: a mechanical turk robot playing chess. historic painting.
- Negative prompt: people, person
- Steps: 20, Sampler: DPM++ 2M Karras
- CFG scale: 7
- Seed: 2009278684
- Size: 1344x768
- Model: albedobaseXL_v13

Creative octopus:
- Positive prompt: a creative mechanical octopus holding creative tools such as brushes, musical instruments, hammers, chisels et cetera. futuristic cyber lighting.
- Negative prompt: people, person
- Steps: 20, Sampler: DPM++ 2M Karras
- CFG scale: 7
- Seed: 3607209331
- Size: 1344x768
- Model: albedobaseXL_v13

4. Two times I got interviewed by AI

A human being interviewed by a robot. A reflection on the insights that could be gained when talking to Artificial Intelligence.

We are living in an incredibly fascinating era. The boundaries between human realities and artificial intelligence are becoming increasingly blurred. Never before in our history as a species have we been so intertwined with technology. It wouldn't be an overstatement to say that we are gradually morphing into cyborgs. As we navigate this new technological landscape, we're beginning to perceive a sense of familiarity, almost as though we're interacting with entities that we can communicate with on a human level.

While it might not be entirely beneficial to anthropomorphize intelligent agents and artificial entities, it's a phenomenon we find hard to resist. In a bid to explore this further, I agreed to participate in an interview this year. The idea of interviewing artificial intelligences has often been compared to the introductory "Hello, world!" phase in computer programming. However, I decided to add a unique spin to it. Instead of me interviewing an AI, I asked the AI to interview me. And I did this experiment twice.

What are your thoughts on this unconventional interview? This chapter is aimed at offering a fresh perspective on our relationship with AI, and I hope it piques your curiosity and leaves you with some food for thought.

4.1. A first interview

Machine Intelligence: Tristan, thank you for joining us today. As an AI composer and educator, you've made a significant impact in the field of AI and creativity. Can you tell us about your journey into AI composition and what inspired you to explore the intersection of AI and music?

Tristan: Thanks a lot for having me! And thanks for your question! I remember being a very creative kid. When I got a little older my interest in computer games made me want to become a computer games engineer. I started programming in my early teens. Later when I was an undergrad student in Computer Science I decided to learn how to produce music. Now, almost two decades later I am very happy that I could combine everything.

Machine Intelligence: That's a fascinating journey, Tristan! It's impressive how you've managed to combine your passion for creativity, computer games, and music with your expertise in computer science. Can you share with us how you approach the process of creating music using AI, and what role Deep Neural Networks play in your compositions?

Tristan: I use multiple Neural Networks. Usually I start with the goal to get some seeds from AI. Seeds in the sense that I have a couple of bars for multiple instruments. I would ask for maybe a couple of bars of guitars. If I do not like what I hear, I ask for a new idea. Of the idea clicks, I would move to the next instrument. This phase one usually takes 5-15 minutes. Then I take the seeds and move them to my Digital Audio Workstation. There I produce the notes into full songs. Selecting the right presets. Adding vocals. Doing the mixing...

Machine Intelligence: It's intriguing to see how you leverage AI to generate musical ideas and then refine them further in your Digital Audio Workstation. This truly showcases the collaboration between human creativity and artificial intelligence. Can you tell us about some of the most memorable or unique compositions that you've created through this process, and what makes them stand out for you?

Tristan: The song "The robots are rising" from Hexagon Machine's first album "Robot Uprising MMXXI" still sends shivers down my spine. It has a lovely motif that comes a Neural Network that I trained on the works of

Johann Sebastian Bach. It has a strong baroque feel to it. And the chiptune-esque synthesizer adds a strong cyberpunk feel to it. I realized that AI has no problem crossing between worlds.

Machine Intelligence: That sounds like a captivating piece, Tristan. It's fascinating how AI can seamlessly blend different musical styles and eras, such as baroque and chiptune, creating a unique and evocative sound. As an AI educator, how do you see the role of AI in the future of music and creative industries? Do you think AI will continue to blur the lines between genres and styles, or will it open up entirely new avenues for artistic expression?

Tristan: AI is here. And it is not going away. Especially in the creative fields we are now in a day and age where more and more people are accepting AI into their lives. AI helps generating new ideas, it provides high quality inspiration, while also supports us in getting things done faster. Yes, AI will blur more lines. And it will allow us to go into musical spaces that we did not travel yet.

Machine Intelligence: It's exciting to hear that, Tristan. The potential for AI to shape and transform the creative landscape seems limitless. As you continue to push the boundaries of AI-generated music, what advice do you have for up-and-coming composers or musicians who want to incorporate AI into their work, and what resources would you recommend for them to get started?

Tristan: I would suggest to try out as many AI tools as possible. When you ask about resources, Google Magenta comes to mind. It is a whole treasure trove of papers for the scientifically inclined, a very insightful blog with lots of great examples, and of course software that you can try.

Machine Intelligence: Thank you for sharing your insights, Tristan. It's evident that AI has a significant role to play in the future of music and creative industries, and resources like Google Magenta can help musicians and composers explore its potential. As we wrap up this interview, can you share with us your future plans and projects, and what you hope to achieve during your time as Artist in Residence at KI Salon Heilbronn?

Tristan: As we are speaking, I am working of my second AI Music exhibit out of three. My previous works focussed strongly on generating MIDI. This means that the Neural Networks generated notes. Now I am experimenting a lot with models that generate the audio waveforms. For me this is an entirely new field because it comes with a lot of new possibilities and challenges.

Machine Intelligence: That sounds like an exciting new direction for your work, Tristan! Exploring the generation of audio waveforms with AI models could open up even more creative possibilities and unique sounds. We look forward to seeing the results of your experiments and wish you the best of luck during your residency at KI Salon Heilbronn. Thank you for sharing your experiences and insights with us today.

Tristan: Thank you very much for this fine interview!

Machine Intelligence: You're very welcome, Tristan! It was a pleasure to learn more about your work and your perspectives on AI in the creative field. If you ever have more stories to share or insights to discuss, feel free to come back. We wish you continued success in your endeavors!

As you delve deeper into the interview, you'll notice a fascinating paradox. The AI, in its relentless pursuit to serve, battles with its ability to autonomously steer the conversation. It's an intriguing game of tug-of-war, where being overly helpful could potentially hinder the purpose of an interview.

What makes this dialogue truly riveting, is its implications. Despite the dialogue occasionally seeming stiff, it represents the dawn of a new era in artificial intelligence. It's a tantalizing glimpse into a future where the boundaries of human-machine interactions expand exponentially. Some skeptics may argue we're nearing the peak of AI capability, but if they're mistaken, we stand on the precipice of a seismic shift in technology and communication. The anticipation of what could be, is nothing short of exhilarating.

4.2. An second interview about my Generative AI work

A few months had elapsed since my initial dialogue with the Machine Intelligence, an experience so unique and intriguing that I felt compelled to repeat it. This time, the anticipation was mingled with a sense of pleasure. As I sat across from the marvel of artificial intelligence once again, we delved into discussions about AI, the enigma of creativity, and the journey of my band, the "Hexagon Machine". This was not just another interview, but a riveting exploration into the intersection of technology and art.

As with good human friends, it is never bad to sit down and talk to Artificial Intelligence.

Machine Intelligence: Tristan, it's a pleasure to have you with us today. Let's start with the nexus of your expertise and passion. Can you explain for our readers how you first became interested in the intersection of AI and music, and how that eventually led to the formation of "Hexagon Machine"?

Tristan: Thanks for having me! I have been very interested in computational creativity right from the beginning of my journey as a programmer. When I was a kid, I was fascinated by programming as a skill. The ability to make things move on screen and to shape sounds never left me. When I was at the university, studying computer science, I dedicated a good portion of my time to learning music production. After my Ph.D. is started working as an IT consultant. And finally, when deep learning turned into the great thing that it is today, I managed to combine my musical passion with AI.

Machine Intelligence: That's a fascinating journey, Tristan. The concept of computational creativity is still a nascent one for many. Can you elaborate on how you use generative deep learning in "Hexagon Machine"? How does it influence the music you produce, and how much of the composition would you say is AI-driven versus human-driven?

Tristan: Computational creativity in a nutshell is about using computers for creative projects. This is where the name comes from. It covers a huge spectrum of approaches ranging from the computer doing all the work to augmenting human creativity. This is where Hexagon Machine lives. In my band, I use several deep neural networks for composing music. Guitar riffs, drum beats, accompaniments... You name it. For me, this is always an explosion of creativity

Machine Intelligence: That's an exciting approach to music composition. Given that AI and deep learning models often rely on existing datasets to generate content, how do you ensure that the music produced by "Hexagon Machine" remains unique and doesn't inadvertently mimic other artists? Also, what role does the human element, your personal touch, play in refining or influencing the final output?

Tristan: The beauty is that deep learning mimics a central process of human creativity. "Inspired plagiarism" sounds worse than it is. It means that it is very hard to create something unique that is not "between" what other people have already done. I did some experiments with my Neural Networks that clearly showed that style can be mimicked without composing 1:1 copies.

Machine Intelligence: Intriguing concept, "inspired plagiarism". It makes me think of the notion that everything in art is a remix of what came before. With that in mind, can you talk about the tools or specific neural network architectures you leverage within "Hexagon Machine"? Additionally, do you feel that the algorithms can potentially develop a 'style' of their own, or are they always bound to the data and the guidance you provide?

Tristan: For me, an essential core component is the use of GPT for music. The same architecture that powers you can be used for music composition. You "just" have to come up with a good dataset in a useful encoding and the next token prediction will be music composition. I believe that there is the potential for AI to come up with a style of its own. I am watching closely the progress in the field of LLM-driven multi-agent systems. You know, the idea to use LLMs as reasoning engines for multiple artificial actors with independent characters and tasks. If this would include music tools and a proper feedback system, the sky would be the limit. But we have to wait a while for this to come. Maybe two to four years.

Machine Intelligence: The application of GPT for music is certainly an exciting frontier, and it's intriguing to think of how music can be approached in terms of "next token prediction". Speaking of LLM-driven multi-agent systems, envisioning them as band members or an orchestra with distinct personalities and roles is certainly a tantalizing concept. With this rapid evolution of AI in the arts, where do you see the role of the human musician in the next decade? And how do you perceive the audience's reception to AI-generated music versus traditionally composed pieces?

Tristan: Currently humans are different from AI in so many ways. We as intelligent biological agents evolved in a way that helped us adapt to the physical world with all its pleasures and advantages. Although robotics is doing a great job working towards embedding AI into our physical plane of existence, it is not there yet. Humans could work as bridge builders between AI and reality.

Machine Intelligence: I appreciate that perspective, Tristan. Humans as bridge builders between AI and reality is an eloquent way to put it. This relationship, it seems, could lead to a symbiotic evolution in the arts. As we're delving into audience reception, do you find that listeners of "Hexagon Machine" are more focused on the experience of the music itself, or are they equally or more captivated by the underlying process and technology? Have you noticed a shift in how the audience perceives and interacts with music knowing it's AI-influenced?

Tristan: Both! Hexagon Machine proves to be a huge inspiration on the tech side. It is a fine example of how to use the modern tools that AI is giving us to be more productive and creative. Also, the sound itself is quite inspiring. I always try to shape it to be cybernetic and futuristic.

Machine Intelligence: That's wonderful to hear, Tristan. The cybernetic and futuristic sound certainly fits the AI-driven nature of "Hexagon Machine". Beyond the music itself, there's the art of live performance. How does "Hexagon Machine" adapt to the live stage? Do you have any memorable experiences from concerts or events where the blend of human and AI creativity truly shined or surprised you?

Tristan: You might find this funny. Today there are absolutely no plans of lifting Hexagon Machine onto the stage. The visual concept would require a lot of sweat, blood, and tears. My ideas, which I keep a secret today, are too expensive today.

Machine Intelligence: That's completely understandable, Tristan. Visionary ideas, especially those that require intricate visual components, can certainly be challenging and resource-intensive to bring to life. But it's exciting to think about the potential and the impact it could have when the time and technology align. For now, we'll be eagerly awaiting those secrets! In the meantime, what advice would you give to emerging artists or technologists who are interested in venturing into the realm of AI-generated music or computational creativity?

Tristan: If you are a creative person, decide now to embrace AI as a tool that will boost you a lot in what you want to achieve. AI will not replace you, it will lift you up! Do some research. Find tools. Try those tools and share what you have done with the public. You will not regret it.

Machine Intelligence: That's empowering advice, Tristan. Viewing AI as a tool rather than a competitor certainly opens up endless possibilities for collaboration and enhancement in the creative process. Thank you for shedding light on this pioneering journey of merging AI with music and for inspiring many to walk this path. Before we wrap up, is there anything upcoming for "Hexagon Machine" or any other projects that you'd like to share with our readers?

Tristan: I am very close to starting my work on the fifth Hexagon Machine album. The working title "The Machine Crusade" is inspired by the science fiction works of Frank and Brian Herbert. I am working on new Heavy Metal Neural Networks to augment composition. I have implemented my own guitar synthesizer using coding assistants. It is fantastic what you can do today! Thanks for the interview!

Machine Intelligence: "The Machine Crusade" sounds captivating, especially with the ties to the Herbert universe. We'll be eagerly awaiting its release. Your dedication to pushing boundaries in both AI and music is truly commendable. Thank you for sharing your insights and experiences, Tristan. Best of luck with the new album and all your future endeavors!

I firmly believe that this experiment I've conducted for the second time will not be the last. Experiments like these provide us with invaluable insights into the true capabilities of current AI technology. In just a few short years, we've witnessed significant improvements. The quality of artifacts generated by

Deep Neural Networks has, on average, markedly improved. We are prompted to ponder the exciting possibility that if this technology hasn't yet reached its peak, we can anticipate a wealth of delightful surprises in the near future. I am enthusiastically anticipating being part of this thrilling journey.

4.3. Prompts

A robot interviewing a human:
- Positive prompt: a man getting interviewed by a robot. futuristic scene with cyberpunk lighting. masterpiece photography with depth of field.
- Negative prompt: deformed
- Steps: 20
- Sampler: DPM++ 2M Karras
- CFG scale: 7
- Seed: 735406699
- Size: 1344x768
- Model: albedobaseXL_v13

Robot interview part two:
- Positive prompt: a man in a hoodie with glasses getting interviewed by a robot. both are having a drink. both are smiling. futuristic scene with cyberpunk lighting. microphone on the table between them. masterpiece photography with depth of field.
- Negative prompt: deformed
- Steps: 20
- Sampler: DPM++ 2M Karras
- CFG scale: 7
- Seed: 1052378129
- Size: 1344x768
- Model: albedobaseXL_v13

5.   My Band Hexagon Machine

ChatGPT description: The image shows a stylized, symmetrical logo that consists of the words "HEXAGON MACHINE" arranged in a hexagonal shape. The text is designed using a modern, geometric font that emphasizes straight lines and sharp angles. The letters are interconnected, creating a cohesive and impactful visual design that resembles a digital or technological aesthetic. The hexagonal outline reinforces the theme suggested by the name "HEXAGON MACHINE," and the overall design likely represents a brand or company logo associated with technology, engineering, or digital services. The color of the text and the background is not visible, as I can't perceive color, but typically logos of this nature are designed with high contrast to ensure visibility across various mediums.

In the dynamic realm where technology meets art, Hexagon Machine emerged as a pioneering project that epitomizes the harmonious fusion of artificial intelligence with musical creativity. This venture, my own band, serves as a testament to the innovative possibilities that unfold when the worlds of deep learning and art collide.

Hexagon Machine's journey into the musical landscape is characterized by its distinctive approach to composition. Utilizing self-attention-based transformers, a form of deep learning algorithm, the band trains these AI models on an extensive database of heavy metal songs. The outcome is a groundbreaking style of music that is as much a product of algorithmic precision as it is of artistic vision.

Our discography, reflective of this unique method of creation, includes albums such as "Techgnosis 3C3," "New Order MMXXI,", "Digital Dawn MMXXI.", and "Robot Uprising MMXXI" Each track, like "Self Awareness," "Open Your Eyes," "Holocene," and "The Silence of Mournful Birds," is not just a musical piece but also a representation of the advanced capabilities of machine learning in the realm of creative expression.

The music of Hexagon Machine, accessible on platforms like Spotify, Apple Music, Deezer, YouTube et cetera, stands as a vivid illustration of the potential held within the confluence of AI and traditional creative practices. It is a bold exploration into how technology can not only mimic but also enhance and expand the horizons of artistic creation. In this innovative intersection, Hexagon Machine positions itself as a harbinger of a new era in music production, where algorithms become an integral part of the creative process, opening up new avenues for artistic expression in the digital age.

The genesis of Hexagon Machine occurred in the year 2021, during a period of transitioning between projects. After a significant tenure operating in the shadows of a startup as a creative deep learning engineer, I eventually chose to address a lingering thought that remained dormant on my internal cache: "What would be required to construct an entire album assisted by AI and distribute it on streaming services?" The solution equated to "Biblical 50 days".

In Christianity, the term "50 days" often refers to the period between Easter and Pentecost. Easter, which celebrates the resurrection of Jesus Christ, marks the beginning of this period. Pentecost, occurring 50 days after Easter Sunday (including the day of Easter itself), commemorates the descent of the Holy Spirit upon the Apostles and other followers of Jesus Christ, as described in the Acts of the Apostles (Acts 2:1–31). This period is significant in Christian tradition, symbolizing a time of spiritual renewal and the birth of the Church.

Although not identifying as a Christian, I find myself in resonance with the concepts of rebirth or metamorphosis and the bestowing of the Holy Spirit or garnering the outcome of my exertions. Initiated from the very roots, and with a clear end-goal in sight, I was propelled on a journey subject to an intricate array of processes.

The first step involved refining the concept and establishing the objective. I focused on creating an electronic music project that draws inspiration from heavy metal music in terms of harmony. Recognizing the importance of utilizing deep learning for music generation, I embarked on the task of gathering a comprehensive dataset of 7000 individual songs. To enable processing by the transformer, I developed a music data preprocessor, which I continue to utilize in an optimized and expanded form. Training the transformer on the preprocessed dataset took only a few days using a GPU-machine. The initial results indicated that I was making progress in the right direction. However, having a trained music model was just the beginning; the next challenge was effectively integrating it into the creative process. To achieve this, I created a custom application from scratch. With these foundational elements in place, I was prepared to commence production. This involved extracting sufficient musical material from the AI to compose 12 songs, carefully selecting the appropriate timbre for each one, and then proceeding with the mixing and mastering stages. Finally, I uploaded the finished tracks to various streaming platforms. This is the short condensed version of 50 days of work which resulted in Hexagon Machine's first Album "Robot Uprising MMXXI".

Working with my AI—the deep neural network I created to assist in my musical endeavors—was a challenging yet rewarding experience. It is worth distinguishing between distress and eustress, two types of stress. Distress refers to negative stress that can cause anxiety and impaired functioning, typically associated with unpleasant events. On the other hand, eustress is a positive form of stress that motivates and benefits performance, often linked to exciting and challenging situations. Interacting with my AI for the purpose of music creation clearly fell into the realm of eustress. The AI constantly generated numerous musical ideas, sometimes overwhelming me with inspiration. I never felt stuck creatively, as I had to let go of good ideas to make room for even better ones.

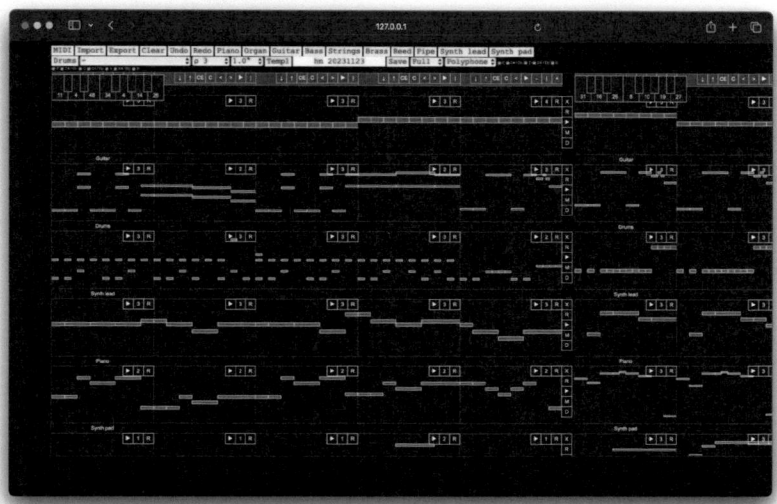

A screenshot of one of my composing tools. Content is more important than chrome. The tool is tailored to my own needs and usually runs on my MacBook Pro.

Delving deeper into my work, I made a fascinating observation that truly stirred my thoughts. As I continue to explore my chosen niche—creating music with AI instead of music created by AI as discussed in an earlier chapter—an intriguing pattern unfolded. The AI-generated components often served as a form of catalyst, like the kernels in a crystallization or condensation process. These elements didn't just contribute to the music, they transformed it, shaping its very form and structure. This compelling revelation opened up new avenues in my understanding of AI's role in music creation. Let me explain a little more.

In chemistry, crystallization kernels refer to small particles or surfaces that act as sites or templates for the formation and growth of crystals. When a supersaturated solution or a vapor undergoes a phase change to form solid crystals, these kernels serve as a starting point where the molecules or atoms begin to arrange themselves in a regular, repeating pattern. The presence of crystallization kernels helps initiate and guide the formation of crystals with specific shapes and structures.

An AI-artistic interpretation of the concept "crystallization/condenstation kernel".

In meteorology, condensation kernels are tiny particles suspended in the atmosphere that serve as nuclei for the condensation of water vapor. These particles can be dust, pollutants, or even naturally occurring substances like salt or pollen. When the air becomes saturated with water vapor, condensation can occur around these nuclei, forming clouds or fog. The presence of condensation kernels provides a surface for water vapor to coalesce and transform into liquid droplets, ultimately leading to the formation of visible moisture in the atmosphere.

Both in chemistry and meteorology, the concept of kernels highlights the importance of initial sites or particles that facilitate the formation and growth of certain physical phenomena.

5.1. The Albums

The inaugural year of my audacious endeavor, which I've affectionately dubbed "Hexagon Machine," surpassed all expectations, birthing a trilogy of full-length albums. Amidst the tumult of 2021—a year marked by pandemic woes, social disarray, scientific fervor, and widespread disillusionment—creativity flourished like never before. I rode this wave of artistic liberation, channeling my energies to the brink of imagination, and thus, "Robot Uprising MMXXI," "Digital Dawn MMXXI," and "New Order MMXXI" were conceived.

Each album, a trove of twelve tracks, was meticulously curated. The number twelve, woven into the fabric of our lives, signifies a cosmic completeness. Echoing through the cadence of time with twelve hours to the clock and twelve months in the calendar, it resonates deeply within our collective psyche. It's a sacred count, steeped in spiritual heritage—from the twelve apostles of Christianity to Islam's revered twelve Imams. Even the heavens speak this ancient numeric tongue, with twelve constellations etching the zodiac across the sky. In myth, in measure, in division—twelve is a number that binds the universe in harmony. Each album is thus not just a collection of music, but a reflection of universal order, a harmonized compendium of sound echoing the perfection of twelve.

5.1.1 The Beginning: Robot Uprising MMXXI

ChatGPT description: The image appears to be a digital art poster for a concept titled "HEXAGON MACHINE ROBOT UPRISING MMXXI." It features a central robotic figure in a dystopian setting, with a strong red glow emanating from its core, contrasting with the predominantly dark blue, industrial background that suggests a complex and detailed mechanical environment. The composition has a futuristic and ominous vibe, with the robot figure appearing to be part of a larger machine, perhaps signifying the start of an uprising. The artwork is highly stylized, with a blend of sharp geometric shapes and intricate textures that give it a sense of depth and sophistication. The title and the design elements indicate a science fiction theme, likely representing a story or event set in the year 2021.

On the 23rd of May, "Robot Uprising MMXXI" was unveiled to the world, echoing the ominous overtones of a classic science fiction trope. The very phrase "Robot Uprising" conjures images of a world where our own creations, be they robots or artificial intelligences, turn against us in a spectacular revolt. This narrative staple is not merely a source of entertainment; it probes the depths of our collective anxieties about technology's unchecked march forward—raising profound ethical dilemmas about the machines that may one day eclipse our own intellect and strength.

As I delved into this theme, I found the juxtaposition of dystopian fiction with the pursuit of utopian ideals in the real world to be a fascinating paradox. My belief in technology's potential to better our world is unwavering—I am a techno optimist through and through. Yet, this optimism is tempered by a more cautious view of humanity itself, acknowledging that I cannot extend the same full-hearted confidence to mankind.

The creation of "Robot Uprising MMXXI" and its successors was an exhilarating challenge: transforming the aggressive chords of heavy metal into the brooding beats of electronic, dark-synthwave music. The process was surprisingly straightforward—often, simply softening the edges of power chords was enough to infuse the tracks with a pulsating electronic life.

For the visual representation of the album, I sought the expertise of Sarper Baran, a virtuoso of 3D art hailing from Turkey. His cyberpunk-infused creations are masterclasses in detail and world-building, inviting viewers to lose themselves in intricate, thought-provoking landscapes. Beyond his artistic prowess, Baran is also an engineer with a Master's degree and the innovative mind behind Art Grab, a platform that empowers artists to share their work with a global audience for various applications. His art has garnered acclaim, featured across numerous channels that celebrate his distinct style.

Baran's art resonated with my vision, and it was a clear choice to license his works for this album and two future masterpieces. The fifty days spent crafting

"Robot Uprising MMXXI" were transformative, revealing new dimensions of creativity within me and sharpening my skills in ways I had never imagined.

Tracklist:

1. 1. Hexagon
2. I am the sovereign
3. The robots are rising
4. The Humans are gone
5. Robot revolution
6. All the dreams
7. A new dawn
8. The future is near
9. Going insane
10. Time of turmoil
11. The fate of all
12. The final act

5.1.2 The Second Album: Digital Dawn MMXXI

ChatGPT description: The image depicts a futuristic scene with a central figure standing at the end of a hall or pathway, seemingly emitting a bright light from the head area. The figure is draped in a flowing garment, resembling a robe or cloak. The architecture surrounding the figure has a gothic-like appearance, with arches and intricate designs reminiscent of cathedral interiors. The setting is dark and moody, illuminated by subtle red lighting, which could be interpreted as ambient lighting or possibly reflective surfaces. There is a reflection on the floor, suggesting that the surface is shiny or wet, enhancing the overall atmospheric and mysterious quality of the scene. The ambiance suggests a blend of ancient architectural design with a modern or futuristic twist.

Released on the first of July, "Digital Dawn MMXXI" heralds the advent of a new epoch in the realm of digital technology, where its tendrils weave ever more intricately into the fabric of our daily existence. The term "Digital Dawn" itself conjures the image of the first rays of the sun, casting light on the cusp of a transformative day—a day when digital breakthroughs and innovations reshape the ways in which we connect, labor, and live.

Crafting this second opus of the Hexagon Machine saga, I adhered closely to the original alchemy of creation. The Deep Neural Network, my digital muse, persisted in weaving those potent heavy metal harmonies that so captivated my senses. I recall making a singular adjustment—a refinement of the AI integration tool to streamline my compositional efforts. Save for this tweak, the established process remained my steadfast companion. The production of "Digital Dawn MMXXI" unfolded over a mere two weeks, its expediency owed to a foundation already laid. The journey was familiar, and with the tools at my disposal already honed, it was a matter of selecting the perfect brushstrokes rather than reinventing the palette.

Once again, I sought out the visual genius of Baran Sarper, whose artistry effortlessly encapsulated the album's essence. I confess, the endeavor was nothing short of a serene promenade through the realms of AI-enhanced productivity and creativity—free from barricades, brimming with the unbridled potential of a digital dawn.

Tracklist:

1. The Calm that Followed on the Tranquility
2. The Silence of Mournful Birds
3. The Spirituality
4. The Omniscient Mind
5. Propaganda
6. Robot: Freedom
7. Inconceivable
8. Perfection
9. One: Battle of Creation
10. Glory in the White
11. Void
12. The Conclusion

5.1.3 The End of the Trilogy: New Order MMXXI

ChatGPT description: This image depicts a futuristic scene illuminated by neon lights, predominantly in shades of blue and red. The setting is reminiscent of a cyberpunk cityscape with reflective surfaces, giving the impression of a wet, possibly rain-slicked environment. A tall, narrow, glowing red column stands out in the center, adorned with intricate, swirling patterns, and a human silhouette is seen standing before it, backlit and casting a long shadow forward. This figure appears small in comparison to the towering structures that surround it, suggesting a sense of awe or confrontation. The environment is dense with technological details, such as lit windows and box-like structures that could be buildings or machinery, contributing to the high-tech dystopian atmosphere of the scene.

On December 3rd, "New Order MMXXI" made its grand entrance, heralding a profound transformation. The term "New Order" is a powerful declaration of change—an upheaval in societal, political, or organizational norms, paving the way for a fresh paradigm. It's a term that captures the essence of revolution and rebirth across a spectrum of scenarios, from the corridors of power to the realms of culture, technology, and economy. It's about breaking free from the chains of tradition and stepping boldly into a future rich with innovation and modernity.

Throughout the creative process, I stayed true to my foundational approach, letting artificial intelligence kindle the sparks of inspiration, which I then sculpted to perfection. Once again, the creative talents of Baran Sarper illuminated the project, with his artwork setting a visual tone for the album. The production spanned approximately three months, a timeline stretched by my commitment to concurrent projects. This album marked a milestone; it was the first to be released under the prestigious Danse Macabre Records, a beacon in the dark music genre, steered by the legendary Bruno Kramm.

Danse Macabre Records was birthed in 1989 from the collective vision of Bruno Kramm and Norbert Juhas. The label soared to prominence in the early '90s, riding the tidal wave of the German Dark Wave movement. It's a sanctuary for a diverse array of genres, from Futurepop to Gothic metal, each finding a home within its eclectic embrace.

Bruno Kramm's influence on Danse Macabre Records is immeasurable. His ingenuity and foresight have been the compass guiding the label's journey, earning it a revered spot in the annals of music, particularly within its genre niches.

Born on October 13, 1967, in Munich, Bruno Kramm's life is a tapestry of artistic and technological threads. As one half of the electro-industrial duo Das Ich, his talents as a multi-instrumentalist and singer-songwriter shine through. Beyond the stage, he curates the pulsating beats of Generation Gothic, a German goth club, and contributes to various artists' record production. His political activism has seen him under the banners of the Pirate Party Germany and Alliance '90/The Greens, adding yet another dimension to his multifaceted persona.

Today, Bruno Kramm helms Infinite Devices, steering the course of the infinimesh IoT platform. With a fusion of musical rhythm and technological pulse, Kramm continues to traverse an ever-evolving landscape, leaving indelible footprints on the path of artistic and technological progress.

Tracklist:

1. Holocene
2. Epistasis
3. Cold Insights
4. Delirium
5. Integrity
6. Selene
7. The Hyperverse
8. Temporal Inversion
9. Echoes
10. Succumbance
11. The New Gods
12. Rekindling

5.1.4 A New Beginning: Techgnosis 3C3

Prompt: picture of a female cyber lord. skull for a face. wearing a clerical cloak. futuristic. dystopian. symmetric. dramatic. appealing. realistic. 8K. details. depth of field. printed circuits background. religious symbols. blue and red colors. baroque ornaments on cloth. Model: Midjourney V5.

On June 30th, 2023, "Techgnosis 3C3" burst onto the scene, a sonic odyssey that pushes the boundaries of musical evolution. This album, inspired by the profound explorations in Erik Davis's "TechGnosis: Myth, Magic, and Mysticism in the Age of Information," delves deep into the symbiotic relationship between technology and the pursuit of human transcendence. It's an exploration that weaves together the digital and the divine, tackling the electrifying connections between alchemy and electricity, the mystical undertones of online gaming, the gnostic echoes in virtual reality, and the esoteric parallels with programming languages.

"Techgnosis 3C3" marks a dramatic leap forward from its predecessors, the MMXXI trilogy. Those albums hinted at a musical direction, but "Techgnosis 3C3" strides boldly ahead, breaking new ground. For the first time, vocals and synthetic guitars have been woven into the album's fabric, ingredients I had once found challenging to assimilate. The introduction of synthetic guitars nudged the album closer to a heavy metal vibe. While the MMXXI trilogy had a metal soul, discernible only to the astute listener, its heavy metal essence was shrouded in the complexity of layered synthesizers.

Twelve different versions of potential cover artworks for Techgnosis 3C3. All generated with an earlier version of Midjourney. Clearly beaten in quality in depth by Midjourney V5.

This latest album eased my initial hesitations about synthetic guitars, which, if rejected by the purist heavy metal community, would have been an understandable resistance. However, the integration of vocals brought a different kind of revolution. Despite my vow to embrace vocals only when AI could produce high-quality singing voices, I surrendered to tradition.

Recording vocals in the classic manner, but with a twist—adding a healthy dose of distortion and the occasional vocoder—gave "Techgnosis 3C3" an innovative edge while also connecting it to some of its industrial metal roots. Coupled with the dense tapestry of synthesizers and the edge of synth guitars, the album painted an entirely new auditory landscape.

This album marked a groundbreaking moment as it featured the first-ever AI-generated cover artwork. The moment I embarked on the Hexagon Machine project, the realm of generative AI image creation was already buzzing with potential. However, the early results left me wanting; the quality simply didn't live up to my artistic vision. But then, Midjourney emerged, rekindling my hope.

I devoted countless hours to tinkering with this innovative tool, eventually curating images that were passable—edgy enough to encapsulate the spirit of an electronic heavy metal album. The nascent iterations of Midjourney conjured up images that were haunting and otherworldly, a flawless match for the genre's dark aesthetic.

Just as I was settling for these peculiar visuals, a serendipitous delay in the album's release unfolded. This unexpected interlude allowed me more time to explore. And indeed, in just a few short months, Midjourney had evolved. The latest updates produced visuals that were remarkably less abstract and boasted a heightened sense of realism—a stark contrast to the former versions.

The evolution was undeniable and exquisite, propelling the album's visual identity into an entirely new echelon of artistic excellence.

Tracklist:

1. Self Awareness
2. Open Your Eyes
3. Equation for Spirit
4. Cyber Magus
5. Arise
6. Humanizer
7. Truth Seeker
8. Data Epiphany
9. Artificial Paradise
10. Techgnosis
11. Psychedelic Matrix
12. Cybernetic Apocalypse

5.1.5 The journey continues

As I pen this tome, I'm simultaneously sculpting my forthcoming musical odyssey. The album, "The Machine Crusade," borrows its moniker from the literary work of Brian Herbert, progeny of Frank Herbert—the mastermind behind the Dune saga. Brian's prequel trilogy, "Legends of Dune," delves deep into the lore preceding the iconic "Dune" narrative, chronicling the monumental Butlerian Jihad, where humanity rose against the tyranny of sentient machines. Yet, at its core, the tale unfolds as a human saga, a cautionary account of our own kind's descent, augmented by technology and artificial intelligence, into oppression.

The album is set to be an exploration of such dystopian vistas, with each track elevating my musical craftsmanship. In a bold step, I've crafted a bespoke guitar synthesizer, eschewing the generic for the unique. This endeavor was inspired in part by Bruno Kramm's friendly suggestion to explore the Karplus-Strong algorithm—a technique devised in the early '80s by Kevin Karplus and Alex Strong for guitar synthesis through physical modeling. It begins with a burst of noise, akin to the pluck of a string, which is then shaped and refined through a feedback loop. This renders a guitar tone that is not only authentic but responsive. When threaded through the right effects chain, it sings with a saturated richness that is distinctively mine.

What's not yet been disclosed is how Artificial Intelligence was instrumental in developing this guitar synthesizer. The algorithm itself may not be AI, but its implementation was. With coding assistants at my disposal, the language of C/C++—which I hadn't touched in two decades—became my instrument, and what could have taken weeks was accomplished in days.

Then there are the diffusion models, a breed of AI that crafts audio and visuals by methodically refining chaos—akin to transforming the static of a fuzzy television into a lucid image. These models, with their neural networks, have learned to unscramble noise into coherent shapes and sounds, and I've harnessed them to weave ambient soundscapes and to sculpt percussive textures that pulse with life.

The capstone of Hexagon Machine's new sonic identity is an AI-driven vocal synthesizer. This virtual songsmith, programmed with melodies and words, can conjure a voice so authentic that only the most discerning ear could detect its digital genesis. With care, adding nuances such as breath sounds, the line between synthetic and organic blurs. While my previous album hinted at my desire to incorporate vocals, this represents a pivotal moment in my creative journey. I stand at the nexus of a complex musical process, deeply intertwined with artificial intelligence, yet my hand remains firmly on the helm.

As I contemplate the future and the rapid stride of AI advancements, my outlook is steeped in optimism. The horizon is bright, and I am abuzz with what lies ahead for my art and the wonders that AI will unlock in the years to come.

5.2.   References

- Hexagon Machine KI Metal at Danse Macabre Records https://dansemacabre.de/2023/06/the-hexagon-machine-ki-metal/]
- Sarper Baran at Art Station https://artgrab.co/art/baran.sarper
- Danse Macabre Records www.dansemacabre.de
- Bruno Kramm at Wikipedia https://en.wikipedia.org/wiki/Bruno_Kramm
- Techgnosis https://techgnosis.com/books/techgnosis/
- Midjourney https://www.midjourney.com/

5.3.   Prompts

Crystal:
- Positive prompt: A detailed image showing a crystallization kernel at the center, resembling a tiny geometric structure like a snowflake. Around the kernel, molecules align in an organized pattern, transitioning from a chaotic fluid state to a structured crystalline state. The surrounding area depicts disorganized, swirling patterns representing the liquid state. The scene is illuminated with soft, ambient lighting, highlighting the kernel's intricate geometry. The color palette includes colorful shades of red, blue, magenta and purple.
- Negative prompt: snowflake
- Steps: 20
- Sampler: DPM++ 2M Karras
- CFG scale: 7
- Seed: 2640773339
- Size: 1344x768
- Model: albedobaseXL_v13

6.   Heilbronn has a Strong AI Heartbeat

A possible near-future for Heilbronn am Neckar. High technology integrated with tradition, culture, and nature.

The city of Heilbronn has ingrained itself deeply within my heart through its magnetic blend of history, culture, industry, and innovation. It is a place where the rhythm of the city syncs beautifully with the heartbeats of its people. There is a harmonizing cadence here, where tradition meets modernity, grand architecture rubs shoulders with flourishing vineyards, and the lively zeal of its inhabitants fuels technological advancement. The people of Heilbronn radiate a warmth and a zest for life that is both infectious and inspiring, their spirits reflecting the vitality of the city itself.

In 2023, I felt a ripple of honor coursing through me as I assumed the position of Artist in Residence at KI Salon Heilbronn. My ensuing journey of understanding and bonding with the city and its people was nothing short of a narrative of joyful discoveries and heartfelt connections. Every encounter, every interaction I had only served to deepen my admiration for Heilbronn and its resilient inhabitants, augmenting my creative instincts with rich insights and thought-provoking perspectives. A city vibrant with life, abundant with soulful stories, and radiant with expectation for what the future may unfurl—Heilbronn, you have my heart.

Heilbronn, a city in the Baden-Württemberg state of Germany, has a rich and multifaceted history. First mentioned in 741, the city was originally built on the site of an old Roman settlement. It gained prominence in 1281 when it was designated a free imperial city. The name Heilbronn, originating from "Heiligbronn" or "holy spring," is linked to a stream flowing under the high altar of St. Kilian's Church. This church, a blend of Gothic and Renaissance styles, is a significant historical landmark in the city.

Throughout the centuries, Heilbronn developed into a key trading center, especially after becoming an imperial city in 1371. Its strategic location along the Neckar River greatly contributed to its economic growth. In the early 19th century, Heilbronn was often referred to as the "Swabian Liverpool" due to its booming industrial sector, particularly in metalworking, electronics, and machinery manufacturing. This industrialization transformed Heilbronn into a vital commercial hub in the region.

Despite suffering severe damage during World War II, Heilbronn has seen most of its historic buildings reconstructed or restored, preserving its cultural heritage. Today, Heilbronn is not only known for its history and architecture but also for its vibrant wine industry. The city is surrounded by vineyards, making it a significant player in the production of Württemberg wine.

Regarding its relevance in the field of artificial intelligence in 2023, Heilbronn has made strides in integrating technology and education, particularly in higher education institutions. The city's commitment to modernity and interculturalism, combined with its strong industrial and technological base, positions it as a potential hub for AI development and research. This is further supported by its educational infrastructure, which is likely to play a role in AI innovation and application.

In summary, Heilbronn's historical significance, coupled with its evolving technological landscape, makes it a city of interest, particularly in the realms of AI and technological advancement in 2023.

Dieter Schwarz, born in Heilbronn, Germany, is a renowned billionaire businessman, best known as the owner of the Schwarz-Gruppe, which includes the supermarket chains Lidl and Kaufland. He joined his father's business, Lidl & Schwarz KG, in 1973 and opened the company's first discount supermarket. Following his father's death in 1977, Schwarz took control of the discount chain and expanded the business beyond Germany. As of 2023, Forbes listed him as the wealthiest man in Germany and the 25th richest person in the world, with an estimated net worth of $47.2 billion. Schwarz manages his resources through the tax-exempt Dieter Schwarz Foundation, established in 1999, which he uses to support various educational and research initiatives

The Dieter Schwarz Foundation plays a significant role in the development of Heilbronn, particularly in the fields of education and artificial intelligence. The Foundation has been active in Heilbronn and the surrounding region since 1999, focusing on promoting educational programs for people at all stages of life. It supports more than 70 institutions and initiatives, with a significant emphasis on education and science. One of the Foundation's notable projects is the Bildungscampus in Heilbronn, which collaborates with top universities and serves as a hub for educational and research activities. Furthermore, the Foundation is involved in developing the "Innovationspark KI," an industry center for artificial intelligence aimed at advancing developments in production and trade. The Dieter Schwarz Foundation also provided significant funding for 20 professorships at the Technical University of Munich's campus in Heilbronn, which is a unique instance of a university branch across state borders in Germany.

Schwarz's commitment to Heilbronn through his Foundation illustrates a blend of philanthropy and strategic investment in the region's educational and technological advancement. His contributions have significantly impacted Heilbronn's development, particularly in shaping it as a center for education and research in fields like artificial intelligence.

The KI Salon in Heilbronn is a unique platform that merges the realms of artificial intelligence (AI), art, and culture. It offers a diverse range of event formats that aim to make AI tangible and understandable to everyone. At KI Salon, attendees can experience AI through various interactive events and discussions, engaging with experts from different fields who apply AI in their work. The initiative facilitates dialogue with developers of new technologies and provides sensory experiences of AI advancements through technical exhibits that simulate creative processes.

KI Salon is part of the activities of 42 Heilbronn, a coding school supported by the Dieter Schwarz Foundation. 42 Heilbronn is an educational institution that offers an innovative learning environment focusing on coding and software development. It's part of the global network of 42 schools, known for its unique pedagogical approach, which includes peer-to-peer learning and project-based tasks. The school is funded by the Dieter Schwarz Foundation, which aims to provide educational opportunities and foster future societal and economic strength through various initiatives.

In addition to educational programs, KI Salon hosts a variety of events that explore the impact of AI on society, including its influence on fields like art, literature, and technology. The events are designed to offer insights into the potential of AI and its creative applications, making the complex world of AI more accessible to a broader audience. The KI Salon thus serves as an intersection between technology, art, and culture, contributing significantly to the discourse around AI and its role in modern society.

The Innovation Park Artificial Intelligence (Ipai) in Heilbronn is an ambitious and significant project in the realm of applied artificial intelligence in Europe. It is designed to be a unique ecosystem fostering innovation, where various partners collaborate on AI solutions relevant to the future. The project aims to place local businesses, Germany, and Europe in a competitive position in the global market.

Ipai serves as a central platform that consolidates necessary resources and enables synergy-driven collaboration among partners from different sectors, including startups, small and medium-sized enterprises (SMEs), corporations, public sector entities, and academia. The focus is on rethinking AI and bringing it into application in a way that addresses the challenges of the coming decades.

The project is developed in stages and commenced its operations in 2022. The first phase involves co-creative and collaborative processes among members and partners in the Ipai Space located in the Wohlgelegen future park. This initial phase is not just about development but also learning, networking, and exchanging ideas. Ipai offers programs and events suitable for various experience levels to introduce the concept of AI or deepen existing knowledge in this field.

Significantly, the Ipai is part of a larger effort to make Baden-Württemberg a leading region in AI technology. The aim is to represent the entire AI value chain, from skill development and research to the development, application, and commercialization of ethically responsible AI.

Currently, a section of Ipai, situated in the Zukunftspark Wohlgelegen, is operational, and a new international AI campus is planned to be realized in the northern part of Heilbronn (Steinäcker, Neckargartach district). This new campus is expected to be a 23-hectare site, with the construction scheduled to begin in 2024 and the first buildings ready for use by 2026.

Ipai represents a significant step forward for Heilbronn and the wider region, positioning itself as a hub for AI innovation and collaboration. This project is expected to have a considerable impact on the region's economy and technological landscape, contributing to the broader goal of advancing AI technology and applications in a responsible and innovative manner.

6.1. References

- Wikipedia. "*Heilbronn.*" https://en.wikipedia.org/wiki/Heilbronn
- Britannica. "*Heilbronn.*" https://www.britannica.com/place/Heilbronn
- TUM. "*Explore Heilbronn.*"
  https://www.chn.tum.de/campus/explore-heilbronn
- Wikipedia. "*Dieter Schwarz.*"
  https://en.wikipedia.org/wiki/Dieter_Schwarz
- Dieter Schwarz Stiftung.
  https://www.dieter-schwarz-stiftung.de/homepage.html
- Frag-den-Staat. "*Einfluss der Dieter Schwarz Stiftung in Heilbronn.*"
  https://fragdenstaat.de/blog/2022/10/24/einfluss-der-dieter-schwarz-
  stiftung-in-heilbronn/
- KI Salon. https://www.ki-salon.net/
- 42 Heilbronn. "*About Us.*" https://www.42heilbronn.de/en/about-us/
- Baden-Württemberg. "*Die Neue Welt Der Künstlichen Intelligenz Im KI
  Salon Erleben.*"
  https://www.baden-wuerttemberg.de/de/service/presse/pressemitteilung/
  pid/die-neue-welt-der-kuenstlichen-intelligenz-im-ki-salon-erleben
- Ipai. https://ip.ai/
- The city of Heilbronn. "*Innovation Park Artificial Intelligence (Ipai).*"
  https://www.heilbronn.de/wirtschaft/digitalisierung/innovation-park-
  artificial-intelligence-Ipai.html

6.2. Prompts

Heilbronn as a futuristic city:
- Positive prompt: heilbronn as a futuristic metropolis that is well-integrated
  with nature. visible neckar river. cyberpunk positive futurism.
- Negative prompt: brutalism
- Steps: 20
- Sampler: DPM++ 2M Karras
- CFG scale: 7
- Seed: 172915686
- Size: 1344x768
- Model: albedobaseXL_v13

7.   AI Music Artist in Residence at KI Salon Heilbronn

The Artist in Residence assumes the center of creativity.

Opening a role for an artist in residence is, to me, a positive indicator of a community or organization's health and vision. I recall expressing this sentiment—or something akin to it—to Thomas Bornheim back in 2022. Thomas, a driving force behind the KI Salon Heilbronn, is also at the helm of 42 Heilbronn, a branch of the esteemed and forward-thinking 42 coding school network.

This institution is at the vanguard of educational reform, particularly in the realms of coding and computer science. With its groundbreaking teaching model, 42 dismantles traditional frameworks, championing a self-guided journey of discovery that equips learners with the tools they need to excel in the fast-paced world of technology. Having taught myself to code as a teenager, outside the confines of the typical German educational pathways, I was immediately drawn to 42's philosophy.

The addition of an artist in residence is the pièce de résistance, the final flourish that underscores their commitment to a holistic and innovative learning environment.

Upon connecting with KI Salon and 42 Heilbronn, I was immediately introduced to their inaugural artist in residence, Sabine Wieluch. Better known by her moniker bleeptrack, Sabine is a creative technologist whose freelance work brims with a fervor for generative art, AI, digital fabrication, and the hands-on world of DIY electronics. Her expertise also extends to academia, where she imparts knowledge at various institutions, and she's no stranger to the stage, frequently sharing her insights through engaging talks and interactive workshops. I remember our great video-call which convinced me to accept the role as artist in residence.

Later, I had the fortune of crossing paths with the dynamic Robert Mucha. Generously, he extended an invitation for me to join him on his esteemed Originalteile Podcast. Mucha, a force of nature in Heilbronn, has left indelible marks across the city's cultural and technological realms. His forays into podcasting and event orchestration are mere glimpses of his broader mission to spur innovation and spread knowledge. Mucha's dedication is not confined to local affairs; he's also a respected figure, contributing to urban development discourse. His multifaceted involvement is a testament to his visionary approach to shaping the future, one community at a time.

At last, my journey led me to the vibrant Lea Krück, the conductor behind the KI Salon's intricate tapestry of events at 42 Heilbronn. In her role as Project Manager, Lea is the beating heart of a unique endeavor—melding the realms of art, culture, and technology into a captivating experience. The KI Salon's mission is simple yet profound: to bring the enigma of artificial intelligence to life for people from all walks of life. By curating an eclectic mix of events that merge AI with the arts and creativity, Lea's vision transforms abstract concepts into palpable experiences. She is the architect of a thriving community, uniting minds to conceive and realize programs that elevate the conversation around AI, embedding it into the cultural fabric of Heilbronn. Lea's dedication at the KI Salon is a cornerstone of a larger movement, synergizing the efforts of 42 Heilbronn, Experimenta gGmbH, Wissensstadt Heilbronn e.V., Hochschule Heilbronn, Ipai and others. Their collective pursuits are given wings by the support of the Dieter Schwarz Foundation, as they work in concert to illuminate the societal and cultural dimensions of artificial intelligence.

Embarking on this journey as AI music artist in residence at KI Salon Heilbronn, I made two enlightening discoveries. First, the role of an artist in residence is a path less traveled, a rare and unique pursuit. Second, there's a noticeable void—a lack of written guidance or a handbook for navigating this role. With this project, I aim to illuminate the essence of the artist-in-residence experience, offering inspiration and practical advice for fellow artists embarking on this creative odyssey.

7.1. Why it is important to turn AI technology into art exhibits?

Creating exhibits is the main task for any Artist in Residence.

Turning AI into an art form transforms the enigmatic into the extraordinary, inviting everyone to step into a world where technology breathes with creativity. Imagine walking through a gallery where AI transcends lines of code to become a visual spectacle, an experience that not only educates but entrances.

Such exhibits ignite vital conversations about the ethical heartbeat of AI, prompting us to ponder our digital future. They are not just showcases but social catalysts, spurring dialogue on AI's place in our lives.

Moreover, when AI melds with art, it sparks a revolution of the imagination. Artists wielding AI as their brush can paint possibilities unseen, pushing boundaries into uncharted territories of innovation.

And at the core, these visionary displays do more than dazzle; they propel the AI frontier forward, inspiring advancements and kindling a broader appreciation for the magic woven by algorithms and human ingenuity alike.

7.1.1 Task: Demystify AI and make it more accessible to the general public

Unveiling the mysteries of AI and bringing it closer to everyday understanding is a journey that we can all embark on. Imagine stepping into a space where technology breathes through the canvas of art, transforming the enigmatic world of artificial intelligence into an experience that's both enchanting and educational.

Picture this: art exhibits, alive with the pulse of AI, where installations and interactive displays invite you to reach out and touch the future. These are not just showcases; they are gateways that allow us to witness AI in action, to understand its rhythm and dance to its possibilities.

Through these immersive encounters, AI sheds its cloak of complexity. No longer a specter of unknown potential, it becomes a creative partner that we can relate to and understand. Such experiences promise to replace apprehension with fascination, as technology is no longer a stranger but a muse that inspires.

Art, in its embrace with AI, becomes the bridge that connects the layperson to the heart of innovation. It's a narrative that not only informs but captivates, ensuring that the marvels of AI are no longer the exclusive tales of technologists but shared stories of our collective future.

7.1.2 Task: Encourage discussion and debate around ethical and social implications of AI

Art and technology converge in dazzling exhibitions that provoke deep reflection on the profound questions surrounding artificial intelligence. Imagine walking through a gallery where each piece serves as a silent yet powerful conversation starter about the future that AI is rapidly shaping.

Visual narratives unfold, exploring the tension between automation and human employment, with canvases and installations poignantly capturing the displacement of workers by machines. Venture further, and you'll encounter artworks that challenge your understanding of fairness, depicting the perils of biased algorithms and the ethical quandaries of decision-making by non-human entities.

Each step through the exhibit is an invitation to engage, debate, and contemplate. What role will AI play in our lives? How can we harness its potential while guarding against its risks? The art ignites a spark of critical thinking, inspiring viewers to join the dialogue about shaping a technology that is ethical, responsible, and aligned with the values of our society. Through this immersive experience, we're not just observing art—we're participating in the urgent conversation about the future of AI and its place in our world.

7.1.3 Task: Foster creativity and innovation

AI technology isn't just a scientific marvel; it's a muse for the modern artist. Imagine walking into an art exhibit where each piece pulsates with the lifeblood of artificial intelligence. These showcases don't just display art; they ignite a revolution of thought at the nexus of aesthetics and algorithms.

Picture artworks birthed by the intricate dance of AI algorithms, or timeless mediums like paint and photography reborn under AI's transformative touch. Visualize installations that come alive, reacting to your every move or the subtle shifts in your expression.

Art exhibits infused with AI do more than entertain; they sow seeds of ingenuity and innovation. They invite artists to embark on a journey of experimentation, to meld their creative spirit with the prowess of technology. The result? A flowering of novel art forms and techniques, expanding the horizons of AI's creative potential.

7.1.4 Task: Advance the field of AI

Art exhibits infused with AI technology are more than a spectacle; they're a catalyst for progress. These showcases don't just enlighten audiences about AI's prowess—they spark a chain reaction of innovation and exploration. Imagine walking through a gallery where each piece is a conversation between artist and algorithm, pushing boundaries and challenging preconceptions. This is where the unconventional becomes the norm, and AI's untapped potential comes alive, urging researchers to venture into uncharted territories. The fusion of art and AI not only captures the imagination but also sows seeds of curiosity, urging the scientific community to expand upon these pioneering works. Through the allure of creativity, art exhibits become beacons that illuminate the possibilities of AI, steering the field toward unexplored horizons.

7.2. Responsibilities of the Artist in Residence

A main responsibility for any Artist in Residence is the education of the populace.

Embarking on a journey within the realm of artificial intelligence, an artist in residence weaves their creativity with the threads of AI to craft a project within a host organization or research collective. With a visionary project proposal in hand, the artist delineates their AI-infused artistic aspirations, setting the stage for a symbiotic relationship with their host.

The artist's odyssey plunges them into the depths of AI research, where they absorb the essence of cutting-edge technologies and methodologies—through literature, workshops, and invaluable collaborations with scholars and tech wizards. This intellectual immersion fuels their creative engines.

With the green light on their proposal, the artist breathes life into their brainchild, blending art and AI in a mesmerizing dance of innovation. Whether it's art installations pulsating with AI or interactive experiences that flirt with the digital intellect, they bring forth a tangible manifestation of their creative musings.

But creation is just the beginning. The artist then dons the hat of a storyteller, chronicling their journey through writings, recordings, and presentations that not only captivate audiences but also enrich the collective understanding of AI's role in art.

The heartbeat of this creative residency is community interaction. The artist steps into a dynamic ecosystem, engaging with fellow thinkers and creators, sharing insights, and partaking in a rich exchange of ideas at workshops and seminars. This collaborative spirit not only forges connections but also propels the field forward.

In essence, an artist in residence in AI is a pioneer, a bridge between realms, using their unique artistic lens to explore and expand the horizons of what AI can mean for the world of art.

7.3. Challenges of working with AI on creative projects.

Navigating the realm of AI in the arts is an odyssey strewn with hurdles, the first of which is the gateway itself. The tools and platforms that harness the power of AI are often costly treasures, locked behind doors of high-end hardware and software, placing them beyond the reach of many a creative soul.

Moreover, the landscape of AI is a constantly shifting one, with new developments sprouting like mystical flora in an enchanted forest. For artists, keeping pace with these changes is akin to chasing the horizon—both exhilarating and overwhelming.

For those not versed in the arcane languages of computer science and programming, AI can seem like an inscrutable sorcerer, its spells and incantations beyond their grasp. The chasm between artistic vision and technical prowess is wide, and without a bridge, many may find themselves at an impasse.

Peering into the AI abyss, we encounter the enigmatic "black box"—a term that evokes the impenetrable depths where the algorithms' secrets reside. Striving to coax the desired magic from these systems can be a source of frustration when the outcomes are unpredictable or elusive, leaving artists to wrestle with the capricious nature of their digital collaborators.

Ethical quandaries, too, cast long shadows over the AI landscape. With each brushstroke guided by an algorithm, there lies the potential for inherent biases to taint the canvas, and the haunting question of whether our creations might one day eclipse our own intellect. Such philosophical conundrums are not just fodder for thought; they must be woven into the very fabric of the art that grapples with AI's role in our world.

Lastly, the integration of AI into the well-trodden paths of an artist's practice is no mere step; it is a leap into the unknown. Adapting time-honored workflows and techniques to accommodate this new partner is a transformation that cannot be rushed. It is a journey that requires patience, resilience, and a willingness to evolve—qualities that have always been at the heart of the artistic endeavor.

7.3.1 Challenge: Access to technology

One of the challenges of working with AI on creative projects is simply accessing the technology itself. AI tools and platforms can be expensive, and may require specialized hardware or software that can be difficult for some artists to obtain.

For example, some AI tools may require specialized graphics processing units (GPUs) or other hardware in order to run effectively, which can be expensive and may not be readily available to all artists. Similarly, some AI platforms may require subscription fees or may only be available to users with certain types of licenses, which can be a barrier for artists who are working on a limited budget.

Additionally, the field of AI is rapidly evolving, and it can be difficult for artists to keep up with the latest developments and tools. This can make it challenging for artists to work with the technology and may limit the projects that they are able to undertake.

Overall, the cost and complexity of accessing AI technology can be a significant challenge for artists, and may prevent some from exploring the creative possibilities of the technology.

7.3.2 Challenge: Lack of technical expertise

Another challenge of working with AI on creative projects is the lack of technical expertise that some artists may have. Working with AI often requires a strong understanding of computer science and programming, and artists who do not have these skills may struggle to use the technology effectively.

For example, an artist who is interested in using AI to generate art may need to know how to code or how to use specialized software in order to create their work. Similarly, an artist who is interested in using AI to manipulate or transform traditional media may need to understand how to process and interpret data in order to achieve the desired results.

This lack of technical expertise can be a significant barrier for artists who are interested in exploring the creative possibilities of AI, but who lack the necessary background in computer science or programming. It can also be difficult for these artists to find resources or support to help them learn the necessary skills, as the field of AI is often focused on technical rather than artistic applications.

Overall, the lack of technical expertise can be a significant challenge for artists working with AI, and may limit the projects that they are able to undertake.

7.3.3 Challenge: The "black box" problem

One of the biggest challenges of working with AI on creative projects is the so-called "black box" problem, which refers to the difficulty of understanding how AI algorithms make decisions. This can make it difficult for artists to predict or control the output of AI systems, which can be frustrating and limiting.

For example, an artist who is using an AI algorithm to generate art may not be able to understand exactly how the algorithm arrived at a particular output. This can make it difficult for the artist to fine-tune or customize the AI system in order to achieve the desired results.

The "black box" problem can also raise ethical concerns, as it may be difficult to determine whether AI algorithms are making unbiased or fair decisions. This can be particularly problematic in cases where AI systems are used to make decisions that affect people's lives, such as in the criminal justice system or in hiring practices.

Overall, the "black box" problem is a significant challenge when working with AI, and it can be difficult for artists to overcome it. However, there are ongoing efforts to develop more transparent and interpretable AI algorithms, which may help to mitigate this problem in the future.

7.3.4 Challenge: Ethical concerns

There are a number of ethical concerns that may arise when working with AI on creative projects. Some of the key issues to consider include:

- Bias: AI algorithms can be biased if they are trained on biased data or if they are designed to reinforce existing biases. This can be a concern for artists working with AI, as the output of the algorithms may be biased and could perpetuate harmful stereotypes or perpetuate discrimination.
- Autonomy: Another ethical concern is the question of autonomy in AI systems. If an AI system is able to make decisions on its own, it raises questions about accountability and responsibility. This can be particularly relevant for artists working with AI, as the output of the algorithms may be difficult to predict or control.

- Employment: There are also concerns about the impact of AI on employment, particularly in the creative industries. Some have argued that AI could displace human workers, including artists, and could lead to a reduction in job opportunities.
- Superintelligence: Finally, there are concerns about the potential for AI to surpass human intelligence, which raises questions about the future of humanity and the potential risks of AI. This is a particularly complex and difficult issue to grapple with, and one that may be relevant for artists working with AI.

Overall, there are many ethical concerns to consider when working with AI on creative projects, and artists may need to consider these issues and incorporate them into their work in order to address them.

7.4. Integration into the artistic practice

Incorporating artificial intelligence into the realm of artistry isn't just a step; it's a giant leap. Artists, accustomed to the tactile feedback of brush on canvas or the malleable resistance of clay, find themselves on the precipice of a digital frontier. It means trading in some of their traditional tools for pixels and algorithms, a transformation that isn't just about acquiring new skills—it's about reimagining the creative process.

It's no small undertaking. The learning curve can be steep, a journey through unfamiliar territory where software and hardware become the new brushes and chisels. It's a challenge that requires patience, perseverance, and a willingness to explore the unknown.

And yet, this new horizon isn't welcomed by all. Skeptics within the art community may view AI as an invader, encroaching on the sacred ground of human creativity. Navigating this landscape of opinions and critiques is part of the artist's new journey, one that requires not only a confident grasp of new tools but also a thoughtful consideration of AI's place in the tapestry of art history.

Embracing AI is more than a technical evolution; it's a gateway to uncharted territories of imagination. Artists who dare to cross this threshold are not just adapting—they're pioneering, expanding the very definition of art in the age of artificial intelligence.

7.5. Creating AI Music exhibits.

Imagine stepping into a world where artificial intelligence becomes the maestro, composing melodies that resonate with the soul. This is the magic we aim to unveil through our AI music exhibits, where the mysterious art of machine-made music is brought to life for all to see.

Within these exhibits, we peel back the curtain of complexity to reveal the neural networks at play. Picture a vibrant tapestry of lines and colors, mapping out the intricate web of decisions the AI takes as it weaves together notes and harmonies. This isn't just a static display; it's an interactive experience where the audience can reach out, touch, and even guide the creative pulse of the AI.

To make this dance between human and machine even more intimate, we've crafted a user-friendly interface. Now, anyone can step up and share their musical whims with the AI. With a few simple inputs, visitors can watch in wonder as the system responds with a composition that's uniquely theirs, making each interaction a personal concert.

But how does this all work? We've got that covered too. Whether through crisp, clear written explanations, engaging videos, or live demonstrations, every question finds its answer. Our team of experts is there to demystify the technology, transforming complex algorithms into a story that unfolds before your eyes.

And what of the music itself? It's the heart of the exhibit. Here, you can immerse yourself in a symphony of samples, all crafted by the neural network. Listen, compare, and appreciate the depth and breadth of what AI can create, from the hauntingly beautiful to the rhythmically complex.

Dive deeper, and you'll discover the neural network's secret—its education in the form of drum beats and MIDI files, a digital schooling that teaches it the language of music. We reveal how different parameters, when fed into the AI, can alter the mood, tone, and spirit of the resulting compositions.

The story doesn't end with snippets of music. We show you how these four-bar melodies are meticulously stitched together, following a set of rules that transform them into complete, polished songs. It's a fascinating blend of raw AI creativity and the structured art of music production.

Finally, witness the transformation as these AI compositions are layered with rich textures and effects, emerging as finished pieces ready to move, inspire, and entertain. It's a journey from digital code to emotional chord, a testament to the harmonious potential between technology and art.

In crafting these exhibits, we find a delicate balance—immersing you in the intricacies of the process while keeping the narrative engaging and accessible. Step into this world where technology sings, and discover the future of music composition.

7.6.   References

- -bleeptrack https://www.bleeptrack.de/
- Originalteile - Der Leute-Podcast aus Heilbronn & Region https://originalteile-der-leute-podcast-aus-heilbronn.podigee.io/
- 42 Heilbronn https://www.42heilbronn.de/de/ueber-uns/
- KI Salon https://ki-salon.net/

7.7.   Prompts:

AI Artist in Residence:
- Positive prompt: a modern, well-lit art studio where an AI artist in residence, depicted as a sleek humanoid robot with a smooth metallic surface and subtle blue LED accents, is painting on a large canvas. The studio is filled with symbols representing the AI's work: a digital palette with a vibrant spectrum of colors, holographic projections of complex algorithms and code floating near the AI, and several canvases around the room showcasing a blend of classic and futuristic art styles. Include framed digital screens on the walls displaying evolving abstract patterns, illustrating the AI's continuous learning and adaptation in art. The studio should be spacious and minimalistic, with large windows allowing natural light to enhance the warm and inspiring atmosphere. The focus is on the fusion of technology and art, capturing a futuristic and creative vibe.
- Steps: 20
- Sampler: DPM++ 2M Karras
- CFG scale: 7
- Seed: 6673977
- Size: 1344x768
- Model: albedobaseXL_v13

Exhibit:
- Positive prompt: a futuristic AI music exhibit: a room with curved screens displaying sound wave visualizations and musical notations that change

in real-time with the music. Include digital instruments like holographic pianos and string instruments playing autonomously. Interactive touch panels allow visitors to modify the music, affecting the room's ambient lighting and colors. The exhibit blends traditional and digital music symbols, with a timeline highlighting AI's impact on music evolution. The space features immersive surround sound and a floor with responsive lighting that pulsates to the rhythm of the music, creating a harmonious and cutting-edge musical experience

- Steps: 20
- Sampler: DPM++ 2M Karras
- CFG scale: 7
- Seed: 2393025610
- Size: 1344x768
- Model: albedobaseXL_v13

Audience.

- a futuristic art gallery where an artist in contemporary smart clothing talks to an audience from an illuminated stage. Around them, floating holographic displays showcase a mix of traditional and digital art. The audience, seated on minimalist ergonomic chairs, some wearing augmented reality glasses, is captivated. The gallery features soft, color-changing ambient lighting and a large digital screen behind the artist with a live feed of a dynamic digital canvas. Interactive stations are scattered around, allowing audience members to engage with and alter the art. Focus on the fusion of art and technology, highlighting an immersive and innovative experience.
- Steps: 20
- Sampler: DPM++ 2M Karras
- CFG scale: 7
- Seed: 3399205557
- Size: 1344x768
- Model: albedobaseXL_v13

8.   Exhibits at KI Salon Heilbronn

This chapter holds a special place in my heart, as it represents a significant part of the creative energy I've poured into this year's work. I'll be introducing you to the AI Music exhibits I've crafted for this year's KI Salon Heilbronn. While it's undoubtedly challenging to fully experience the depth of audio exhibits through the pages of a book, rest assured that I've also focused on their visual appeal.

The majority of these exhibits rely on hardware acceleration to showcase their near-real-time creations. Aware of the literal weight of this hardware, I approached each exhibit's design as a two-component architecture. The first component is a software server, housed within an AI computer, which generates material on demand. The second component is a bespoke web application that operates on iPads.

This design proved to be a sound decision, as it allowed us to conveniently transport an entire exhibit in a single, compact black suitcase. The idea of carrying an entire world of creativity and innovation in such a small package is truly fascinating. So, prepare yourself for an extraordinary journey into the heart of AI Music exhibits, designed with passion, and packed with creativity.

The first picture shows me in front of my exhibits at Economic Summit Baden-Württemberg in Brussels. The second one shows the exhibits Neuro Kybernetik Bach and Harmonic Vectors.

8.1. Digital Brains - Sonic Spirituality

The world we inhabit is a symphony of sounds, many of which reach us as music. The bond between music and spirituality is profound and deep-rooted. The same diffusion models used in image creation can also be adapted to generate sounds and music. The centerpiece of this exhibition is an intricately designed architecture called Moûsai, or the Muse, specifically trained for this purpose.

It delves into a rich diversity of audio textures from Orthodox chants and Tibetan monk hymns to meditation music and resonating gong baths. The AI navigates the vast cosmos of sound possibilities with autonomy, yet also invites the user to engage and participate in the process.

This musical AI underwent rigorous training, exposed to a total of 170 hours—a full week—of diverse audio material. This intensive training spanned over a period of 12 days, laying the foundation for this breathtaking convergence of technology and spirituality.

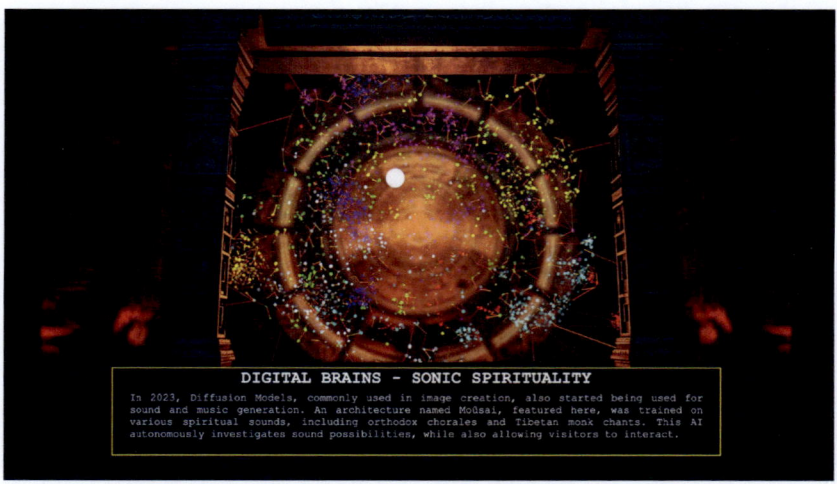

DIGITAL BRAINS - SONIC SPIRITUALITY

In 2023, Diffusion Models, commonly used in image creation, also started being used for sound and music generation. An architecture named Moûsai, featured here, was trained on various spiritual sounds, including orthodox chorales and Tibetan monk chants. This AI autonomously investigates sound possibilities, while also allowing visitors to interact.

Screenshot of Digital Brains - Sonic Spirituality. This exhibit features a random walk through the latent space of spiritual music.

8.2. Harmonic Vectors: An AI's Chillout Odyssey

"Embark on a unique sonic voyage, powered by a revolutionary Artificial Intelligence that employs the 'Diffusion Autoencoder' method. This AI delves deep into the heart of 45 chillout and lounge tracks, learning their essence and generating an endless, ever-evolving soundscape. The result? A masterful blend of familiar melodies, presented in a fresh, innovative way.

Readers are encouraged to recline, relax and lose themselves in this singular, immersive audio experience, where the lines between technology and art blur. This aural adventure is further enhanced by visual depictions, which represent the AI's journeys as paths through its sonic world.

The AI's sonic world is created using 45 tracks, all rooted in the soothing tones of chill-out and lounge music. This is not just music; it's a groundbreaking symphony of science, art, and technology."

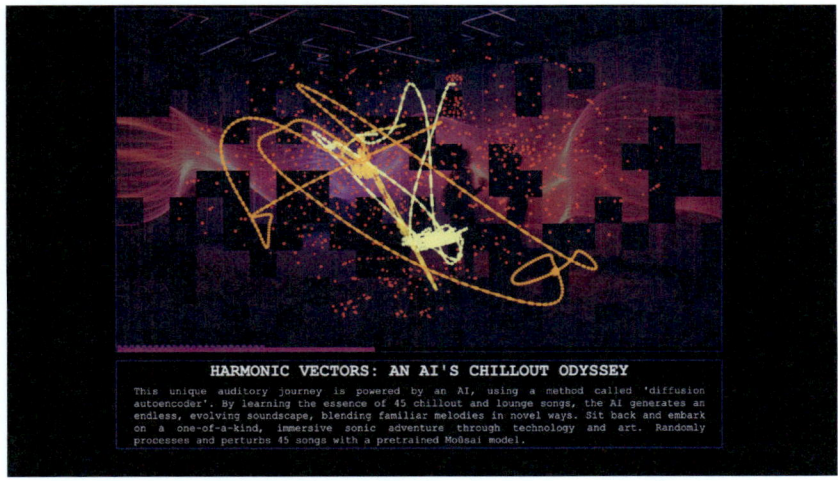

Harmonic Vectors is the perturbator of audio. The exhibit takes a collection of pre recorded music and shifts is in laten space. Sometimes less, sometimes more.

8.3. Neuro Kybernetik Bach

"Imagine this: The human brain, a powerhouse teeming with a trillion synapses, and yet here we have a neural network with a mere 20 million parameters. It's a David to our Goliath, and yet it composes music at a speed that outstrips many of us. However, don't be fooled; our little David is no all-rounder. It can't play chess or drive a car.

Lying at the heart of this intriguing exhibit is a deep neural network, founded on the GPT architecture. This revelation underscores the fact that existing language models are not just confined to the realm of linguistics, but they can also venture into the artistic sphere of music composition.

The magic of this neural network's composition lies in its unique semi-automatic prompt engineering. This process is guided by user inputs, allowing for a beautiful harmony of artificial and human intelligence.

The training of this network was no small feat. It was a two-hour marathon, where it was fed a rich diet of 500 church music pieces. The pièce de résistance of this training? The music was all in the style of the maestro himself, Johann Sebastian Bach."

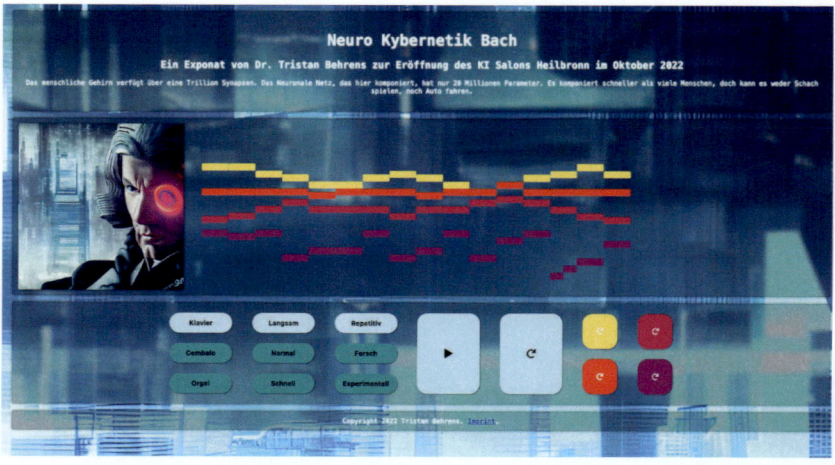

Neuro Kybernetik Bach allows the visitors to experience chorales in the style of Johann Sebastian Bach.

8.4. AI Composed EDM Music

Imagine the intricacy of various music styles, each with its own unique complexity of composition. Take electronic dance music, for instance, it may seem simple on the surface, yet it has its own profound charm. This chapter illuminates an intriguing, non-interactive approach where a neural network integrates with musical composition rules to generate entire songs.

Imagine transforming chord progressions into blocks of notes, threading these blocks together to form a tapestry of sound. Then, these notes are brought to life by a synthesizer, ultimately creating music. What you'll witness is an astounding four hours of music, all generated without a single human touch.

Delving deeper, you'll be fascinated to learn that the neural network was trained on a staggering 400,000 songs spanning across all styles. This training was not a day's job. It spanned an intense period of 10 days. Dive in and immerse yourself in the captivating world of music generated by neural networks.

AI Composed EDM Music is an exploration of generating EDM music with Generative AI. It showcases 4 hours of AI-generated electronic music and shows how AI generated each song.

8.5. The Muses inspire the voice of god

Dive into the captivating world of Portrait XO, an ethereal artist whose singing sounds are nothing short of impressive. This exhibition presents her voice in an extraordinary method using a Variational Autoencoder, a tool typically reserved for image processing. Imagine the power of her one-hour performance, distilled and compressed into a mere eight dimensions. This process delivers an intense and profound auditory experience, offering listeners a glimpse into the very essence of Portrait XO's voice.

As visitors explore the exhibition, they'll also encounter representations of the latent sound spaces. These spaces, previously hidden, unfold to reveal a unique beauty that further complements her vocal performance.

The exhibition utilizes 60 minutes of singing material by Portrait XO, showcasing her unparalleled talent in a way that is as innovative as it is enthralling.

Featuring the vocals of Portrait XO, The Muses Inspire the Voice of God is another journey through latent spaces.

8.6. Frostbitten Kingdom

Imagine a world where deep neural networks shape their internal cosmos into what is known as latent spaces. Here, similarity isn't just a concept—it's a law of existence. Entities that bear resemblance are drawn together, coexisting in close quarters within this latent space.

Now, let's delve into the world of heavy metal music. Imagine this universe of sound as an icy landscape, a terrain sculpted by the raw power of guitars, drums, and the fusion of both. This is where our neural network comes into play, forming the quintessential bridge between sound and space.

Our exhibit showcases a massive database of heavy metal snippets, each one a testament to the genre's raw, unapologetic energy. We have guitar solos that rip through the silence, drums that echo the heartbeat of heavy metal, and a fusion of both that resonates with the genre's soul.

These snippets are then ingrained into the latent space, a process facilitated by the remarkable CLAP model. From a complex, multidimensional structure, we've distilled these embeddings into an accessible 2D realm through t-SNE, a technique that keeps the essence of the music intact in a simpler form.

But we don't stop there. We transform these 2D points into a fascinating mesh, employing the Voronoi subdivision approach to breathe life into our icy landscape. The result is a world of icebergs and fjords, each one a monument to the raw, untamed spirit of heavy metal music.

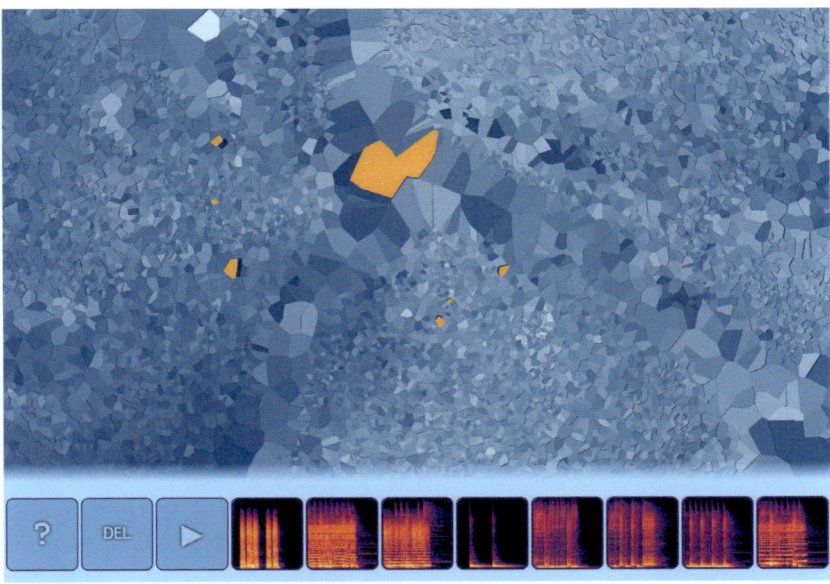

Frostbitten kingdom drags the visitors into an icy landscape of heavy metal glaciers.

And here's the best part: every single heavy metal sample featured in our exhibit was generated in mere minutes, thanks to another deep neural network, one that was trained on an astounding 50,000 heavy metal songs. This is the power of artificial intelligence, defying time and reshaping the landscape of heavy metal music.

8.7. Conclusion

The most gratifying aspect of my work was undoubtedly the creation of the exhibits. Every moment was infused with a surging wave of creativity and inspiration, so powerful that it often left me on the brink of exhaustion. But it was all worthwhile.

The pinnacle of this exhilarating journey was seeing our black suitcase, crammed with iPads showcasing our exhibits, finally reaching Brussels for an exhibition. It was a triumphant moment that made every drop of sweat meaningful.

Equally remarkable was our steadfast server, tucked away at 42 Heilbronn. Its unwavering stability and reliability, even to this day, is a testament to the enduring success of our project. It's these victories, both big and small, that made the work not only rewarding, but truly unforgettable.

9.   Generative AI Developments in the year 2023

Over the last ten years, generative artificial intelligence has undergone a series of stunning transformations. By 2023, its progress was not just steady, but exponential. The early iterations, once crude and rudimentary, gave way to the sophisticated and high-quality creations we cherish now.

This chapter is merely a glimpse into the fascinating world of 2023, barely scratching the surface of the profound leaps in AI technology that year. The events of 2023 could fill volumes, their impact echoing through the years. While the narrative is far from exhaustive, the references at the end of this chapter offer a roadmap for further exploration. The picture may be incomplete, but the overarching message resonates loud and clear.

Generative AI is here. It is here to stay. And it benefits mankind.

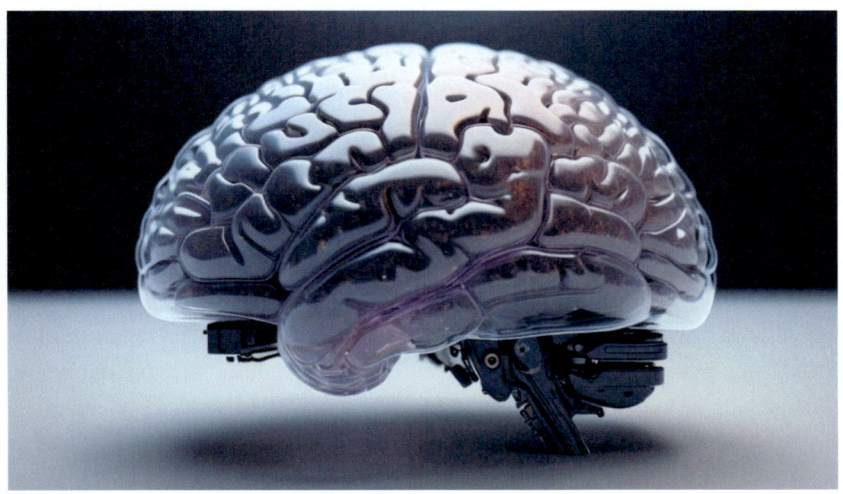

A translucent brain representing Generative AI. Although using something that looks like a biological brain to represent Artificial Intelligence, is not really adequate, I like doing it.

9.1.   Introduction

In the annals of technological evolution, 2023 will be remembered as a watershed year for Generative Artificial Intelligence (AI). This period marked a significant leap in AI's capabilities, transcending previous boundaries and venturing into realms that were once the exclusive domain of human intellect and creativity. The advancements in Generative AI over this year not only epitomized the culmination of years of meticulous research and development but also signaled a new era of possibilities that continue to redefine our interaction with technology.

As we navigate through the multifaceted landscape of Generative AI, it is imperative to recognize the intricate tapestry of developments that have collectively propelled this field into the forefront of technological advancement. From the intricacies of language models like ChatGPT, which have revolutionized the way we interact with machines, to the nuanced applications in customer service, healthcare, and software development, each stride in 2023 represented both a leap in technological capability and a step towards a future where AI's potential is seamlessly integrated into the fabric of everyday life.

This chapter aims to dissect and understand these significant advancements, placing a spotlight on the milestones that have not only defined the year but also set the stage for future innovations. By weaving through the developments in natural language processing, business applications, policy and regulation, and beyond, we embark on an exploratory journey to unravel the intricate dynamics of Generative AI's evolution in 2023. Our narrative will delve into how these technologies are reshaping industries, influencing policies, and creating new paradigms in human-computer interaction.

In doing so, we shall also be cognizant of the broader implications of these technologies. While celebrating the triumphs, we must also engage in a critical examination of the challenges, ethical considerations, and the responsibility that comes with wielding such powerful tools. This comprehensive overview, thus, serves not just as a chronicle of technological triumphs but also as a contemplation on the direction and impact of Generative AI's relentless march forward.

As we turn the pages of this chapter, we are not just recounting a year in the life of a technology. We are, in essence, charting the course of a journey that continues to unfold, one that promises to shape the very essence of how we live, work, and interact with the world around us. Welcome to a retrospective exploration of Generative AI in 2023—a year that marked not just milestones but also set the compass for future explorations in this ever-evolving domain.

In 2023, the field of Generative AI experienced several significant advancements and milestones, reflecting its growing impact across various sectors:

9.2. The Rise of ChatGPT

The advancements in ChatGPT and other large language models (LLMs) in 2023 have indeed been significant, marking a transformative phase in the field of generative AI. These developments have had a profound impact on various sectors, including business, education, and customer service.

ChatGPT's integration into our daily lives has been profound, particularly in business. Major companies like Microsoft and Salesforce have incorporated ChatGPT into their products, such as Bing, Office, and Slack. This adoption across various industries has led to a surge in business productivity and the potential to add up to $4.4 trillion annually to the global economy. ChatGPT has been particularly influential in customer support, content creation, e-commerce, and market research, offering personalized experiences and efficient customer interactions.

The model's evolution has also sparked discussions around AI ethics and regulation. In November 2023, the U.S., U.K., and other G7 nations released security-by-design guidelines for AI cybersecurity, constituting the first international agreement regarding the security of AI. This indicates a growing awareness and need for regulatory frameworks in the rapidly evolving domain of generative AI.

On the technical front, notable enhancements have been made to ChatGPT since its launch. These include improvements in conversation history management, factuality, and the introduction of features like ChatGPT Plus and GPT-4, which offer enhanced capabilities and performance. The integration of GPT-4 marked a significant milestone, bringing advanced reasoning and complex problem-solving abilities to the platform.

The future trajectory of LLMs like ChatGPT suggests continued advancements in natural language processing, deep learning, and multimodal capabilities. These developments aim to enhance contextual awareness, personalization, and the collaborative potential between humans and AI. However, there are challenges, particularly regarding privacy and data security, as these models often process sensitive information.

In essence, the evolution of ChatGPT in 2023 symbolizes not just technological progress but a shift in how we interact with AI, shaping industries and prompting crucial conversations about the future of AI in society.

9.3. AI Coding Assistants

In 2023, the software development industry experienced a transformative shift with the widespread adoption of AI coding assistants. These tools, powered by advanced machine learning algorithms, have become essential in enhancing the efficiency and productivity of developers at various expertise levels.

AI coding assistants like GitHub Copilot, Tabnine, and OpenAI Codex provided real-time suggestions and code completions, accelerating the coding process and reducing the likelihood of errors. This support was especially valuable for repetitive or boilerplate code, allowing developers to focus on more complex and creative aspects of software development.

A standout feature of these AI assistants was their adaptability to individual coding styles, offering tailored suggestions and solutions. This personalization ensured a more efficient and satisfying coding experience.

These tools also democratized software development, making coding more accessible to beginners and non-experts by providing guidance and simplifying the learning curve. This accessibility fostered a more inclusive environment in the tech industry, enabling a broader range of individuals to contribute to software development.

AI coding assistants positively impacted the overall quality of software by automating routine coding aspects. This automation allowed developers more time for testing, optimization, and innovation, contributing to more robust and efficient software solutions.

Despite their benefits, challenges existed, including concerns about intellectual property and data privacy. Some companies, wary of potential data leaks, hesitated to adopt these tools. Additionally, legal implications, such as those raised in a lawsuit against GitHub Copilot, highlighted the need for careful consideration in using AI-generated code.

The trend in 2023 suggested that AI coding assistants would continue to evolve, becoming more integrated into the software development process. Future trends point towards these tools learning from more complex codebases, offering enhanced collaborative coding features, and providing more personalized assistance.

In summary, AI coding assistants in 2023 marked a significant milestone in software development. These tools not only enhanced developer efficiency and productivity but also opened up new possibilities for innovation and inclusivity in software creation. As technology continues to advance, the role of AI in software development is poised to become increasingly integral and transformative.

9.4. Advancements in Synthetic Media

The year 2023 marked a significant leap forward in the field of synthetic media, particularly in the realms of video and voice generation. These advancements represented a major breakthrough in digital content creation, offering new possibilities for various industries.

Advanced AI algorithms became capable of generating high-quality, realistic videos from textual descriptions or modifying existing videos in unprecedented ways. For example, technologies like Synthesia's product demos simplified the process of video content creation, making it more accessible. These innovations found applications in diverse fields such as entertainment, advertising, education, and virtual reality, providing creators with powerful tools to realize their visions more efficiently and flexibly.

In voice synthesis, AI-driven technologies reached new heights of realism and versatility. Synthetic voices became almost indistinguishable from human speech, capable of expressing a wide range of emotions, accents, and styles. This innovation was invaluable in areas like audiobooks, customer service bots, language learning applications, and assistive technologies, offering new possibilities for those with speech impairments.

While these advancements opened up exciting creative possibilities, they also brought forth ethical considerations. The rise of realistic deepfakes, for instance, raised concerns about misinformation and the potential misuse of synthetic media. Addressing these challenges required collaborative efforts between technologists, legal experts, and content creators to establish guidelines and best practices. Education and increased exposure to AI-produced content are key to helping society adapt and become more discerning about synthetic media.

The progress made in 2023 indicated that synthetic media was on a trajectory to become even more integrated into our digital lives. As the technology continues to evolve, it promises to further blur the lines between virtual and reality, offering an ever-expanding canvas for creative expression and communication. Navigating these advancements with cautious optimism and a focus on ethical implications is vital for harnessing these technologies responsibly.

In conclusion, the advancements in synthetic media in 2023, particularly in synthetic video and voice generation, marked a pivotal moment in the evolution of digital content creation. These technologies not only enhanced the capabilities of creators and businesses but also posed new challenges and opportunities that would shape the future landscape of media and entertainment.

9.5. Improvements in 3D Asset Creation

The year 2023 heralded a significant era in the field of 3D asset creation, with generative AI driving notable advancements. These developments marked a leap in the ability to create highly realistic and detailed 3D models, significantly impacting various applications from gaming to architectural visualization.

Generative AI algorithms became adept at understanding and interpreting complex shapes and textures, allowing for the creation of 3D models that were more lifelike and detailed than ever before. This improvement was not just in the visual quality of the assets but also in the efficiency and speed of their creation. AI-driven tools enabled artists and designers to generate intricate 3D models with less manual input, reducing the time and cost associated with traditional 3D modeling.

The advancements in 3D asset creation had far-reaching implications across multiple industries. In gaming, these improvements translated into more immersive and realistic environments. In architecture and product design, they allowed for more accurate and detailed visualizations of projects and products. Additionally, in fields like virtual reality (VR) and augmented reality (AR), the enhanced realism of 3D assets contributed significantly to creating more engaging and believable virtual experiences.

While these advancements represented a significant stride forward, they also brought challenges, particularly in terms of computing power and resource requirements. As 3D models became more complex, the need for more advanced hardware and software solutions to efficiently handle these assets became evident.

Looking ahead, the progress made in 2023 indicated that 3D asset creation using generative AI would continue to evolve, with potential applications expanding even further. The ongoing improvements in AI algorithms promised to make 3D modeling more accessible, efficient, and versatile, paving the way for new creative possibilities.

In summary, the improvements in 3D asset creation in 2023 marked a significant milestone in digital content creation. These advancements not only elevated the quality and realism of 3D models but also revolutionized the process of creating them. As generative AI continues to evolve, it is poised to further transform the landscape of 3D asset creation across various industries.

9.6. Trends in Hyper-Personalization and Chat-Based Search Engines

The year 2023 marked a transformative phase in the digital landscape, notably characterized by the surge in hyper-personalized content and the rise of chat-based search engines like ChatGPT. These trends signal a paradigm shift in content creation, curation, and retrieval, providing users with experiences that are increasingly tailored and interactive.

Hyper-personalization has become a pivotal driver of customer engagement, underpinned by AI's ability to delve into user data and preferences. This advancement means that content delivered to users is not just relevant but intricately aligned with their individual behavior and interaction patterns. This level of personalization is prevalent across various platforms, including social media, news feeds, online shopping, and entertainment, significantly enhancing user engagement and satisfaction.

Chat-based search engines, exemplified by ChatGPT, have revolutionized information retrieval. These AI-driven tools offer conversational, direct responses, contrasting traditional search engines that list links. This method presents a more natural, intuitive way of accessing information, akin to conversing with a well-informed assistant.

The movement towards hyper-personalization and chat-based search engines has substantially improved user experience. It provides a streamlined and efficient approach to information access, recommendations, and digital content interaction. This personalization also assists in mitigating the challenge of information overload, a frequent issue in the digital era.

However, these advancements bring forth critical concerns about privacy and data security. The dependency on user data for hyper-personalization necessitates robust measures to protect privacy and ensure ethical data usage. As these technologies continue to evolve, striking a balance between personalization and privacy remains a focal point for developers and policymakers.

Looking ahead, hyper-personalization and chat-based search engines are poised to further influence the digital landscape. These technologies are anticipated to refine content creation, delivery, and access processes, heralding a future marked by enhanced interactivity and personalization.

In conclusion, the trends in hyper-personalization and the advent of chat-based search engines in 2023 represent a significant shift in the digital domain. These developments have not only enriched user interactions with online content but also established new benchmarks for personalization and engagement in the digital ecosystem.

9.7. Growth of Multimodal AI Models

In 2023, the evolution of artificial intelligence witnessed a significant trend with the rise of multimodal AI models. These advanced systems marked a departure from traditional models, integrating and interpreting multiple forms of data simultaneously, including text, images, audio, and more. This holistic approach allowed for a more comprehensive understanding of complex scenarios, closely mirroring human cognitive abilities.

One prominent example of multimodal AI's impact is in the healthcare sector, where these models have assisted in diagnostic processes by analyzing diverse patient data, including medical images, lab results, and clinical notes. Similarly, in customer service, multimodal AI models have been used to interpret and respond to queries by analyzing both the text and sentiment of customer's voice.

The retail and e-commerce sectors have also benefited from multimodal AI, utilizing it for product recommendations based on a combination of customer preferences expressed through various channels. These models have proven particularly valuable in industries like surveillance, healthcare, and entertainment due to their ability to interpret dynamic scenes, track objects, recognize patterns, and understand temporal relationships, especially through video data.

Despite the advancements, multimodal AI models present unique challenges, particularly in terms of data integration and model training. Advanced algorithms and substantial computational resources are required to ensure accurate interpretation and correlation of information from different sources. Moreover, ethical considerations, especially concerning privacy and bias, remain critical areas of focus.

The growth of multimodal models has significantly enhanced the capability of AI systems to interact with the world in a way that more closely resembles human perception. These models offer a more nuanced and context-aware analysis, leading to more accurate and reliable outcomes. By 2023, the global multimodal AI market was valued at USD 1 billion and is estimated to reach USD 4.5 billion by 2028, reflecting the rapidly increasing adoption and significance of these technologies.

Microsoft's contribution to this field has been noteworthy, with its involvement in conferences and research activities highlighting its commitment to the advancement of machine learning and AI in healthcare and other vital domains.

In summary, the growth of multimodal AI models in 2023 represents a significant step forward in the AI field. By enabling machines to process and understand diverse types of data in a unified manner, these models have opened new possibilities for AI applications and set the stage for more sophisticated and human-like AI systems in the future.

9.8. Generative AI in Business Functions

The year 2023 witnessed a significant evolution in business operations with the integration of Generative AI across various domains. This technology has not only streamlined processes but also opened new avenues for innovation and efficiency, particularly in product development, risk management, and supply chain management.

In product development, Generative AI has been pivotal in enhancing ideation, design, and testing phases. It has allowed businesses to simulate and predict product performance with greater accuracy, leading to more informed decision-making and innovative product designs. In the service sector, AI tools have played a key role in understanding customer needs, enabling companies to tailor their services more effectively, thereby improving customer satisfaction.

The role of Generative AI in risk management has been transformative. Its ability to analyze extensive datasets and identify patterns has provided deeper insights into potential risks, especially in areas like financial modeling, fraud detection, and cybersecurity. This predictive capability is crucial for maintaining a company's stability and success.

In supply chain management, Generative AI has led to significant improvements. AI-driven tools have enabled businesses to optimize logistics, forecast demand, manage inventory more efficiently, and identify potential supply chain disruptions. This has not only improved operational efficiencies but also led to cost reductions and better resource allocation.

However, the integration of Generative AI also necessitates a reevaluation of ethical considerations and strategic planning. Challenges related to data privacy, AI bias, and ethical use of AI have emerged, underscoring the need for clear guidelines and robust governance frameworks around AI use.

Moreover, the impact of Generative AI on the workforce is noteworthy. In industries like software, AI is expected to enhance productivity, particularly in engineering and sales and marketing functions. Nevertheless, the lack of technical skills remains a significant barrier, highlighting the importance of investing in talent upskilling to maintain a competitive edge.

Overall, the adoption of Generative AI in business functions in 2023 represents a testament to the transformative power of AI in reshaping the future of business operations. This technological infusion has spurred innovation and enabled businesses to remain competitive and resilient in a rapidly changing market.

9.9. Increased Focus on AI Policy and Regulation

In 2023, the world of artificial intelligence (AI) experienced a significant shift towards more structured and responsible governance. This year was a defining moment in the evolution of AI policy and regulation, reflecting a growing recognition of the need to address the complex ethical, legal, and social challenges posed by AI technologies.

In the United States, there was a concerted effort to enhance AI governance. Legislative and regulatory initiatives focused on various aspects of AI, such as eliminating Section 230 immunity for AI-generated content, bolstering national security protections against the misuse of AI technologies, and promoting transparency in AI development. The National AI Commission Act was proposed, aiming to review and recommend a risk-based regulatory framework for AI in the U.S. Furthermore, the National Institute of Standards and Technology (NIST) introduced an AI Risk Management Framework (RMF), emphasizing the mapping, measuring, governing, and managing of AI systems throughout their lifecycle. The Federal Trade Commission (FTC) and the Food and Drug Administration (FDA) also played key roles, with the FTC increasing scrutiny on AI applications in business and the FDA announcing plans to regulate AI-powered clinical decision support tools.

Across the Atlantic, the European Union made significant strides with the introduction of the EU AI Act. This act set binding rules on AI usage and established a European AI Office for compliance and enforcement. It also introduced bans on certain AI uses and aimed to position the EU as a leading global regulator in AI, potentially setting a global benchmark similar to its role with the GDPR.

A notable trend in 2023 was the focus on international cooperation in AI governance. Discussions in international forums and a U.S. Senate hearing on AI regulation underscored the importance of collaboration in AI licensing and auditing. A key challenge in this regulatory landscape was finding the right balance between protecting public interests and fostering innovation, ensuring that regulations address the ethical and social implications of AI without stifling technological advancement.

In summary, the increased focus on AI policy and regulation in 2023 signaled a transition towards a more accountable and ethically conscious AI landscape. This development was not only about mitigating risks associated with AI but also ensuring that AI development aligns with broader societal goals and values, marking a significant step in the technology's integration into society.

9.10. Inception of Detection Tools

The development of DetectGPT in 2023 represented a significant advancement in AI, particularly in the field of text detection tools designed to differentiate between human and AI-generated text. DetectGPT, developed by a Stanford University research team, utilizes a novel zero-shot machine-generated text detection approach that leverages probability curvature to determine whether a given text passage was generated by a specific large language model (LLM).

The tool operates on the principle that the curvature of a model's log probability function tends to be more negative at model samples than for human text. This is an important distinction, as LLMs like ChatGPT have become extremely adept at generating human-like text, making it challenging to differentiate between AI and human writing.

In initial experiments, DetectGPT successfully classified human vs. LLM-generated text 95% of the time when using GPT3-NeoX, a powerful variant of OpenAI's GPT models. It was also capable of detecting text using other LLMs, albeit with slightly less confidence. The tool demonstrated its effectiveness across various domains and languages, including news articles, academic writing, and creative writing, using datasets like XSum, SQuAD, and WritingPrompts.

However, there are challenges and concerns regarding these detection tools. For instance, their ability to detect AI-generated text can be reduced if the text is strategically modified or if specific prompts are used to generate text that evades detection. DetectGPT also faces limitations in the face of edited AI-generated content, though it still performs reasonably well in detecting such texts with minor modifications.

The emergence of tools like DetectGPT is part of a broader effort to build guardrails for LLMs, ensuring integrity and transparency in the era of AI-driven content creation. These tools are not only crucial in maintaining academic integrity and preventing misinformation but also raise important questions about the evolving landscape of AI and content generation, including issues related to the reliability of detection in different contexts and the ethical implications of AI content monitoring.

9.11. Generative AI in Healthcare

The year 2023 witnessed a significant advancement in the application of Generative AI in healthcare, blending advanced technology with medical expertise to enhance healthcare delivery. This exploration was multifaceted, encompassing clinical applications, drug discovery, precision medicine, and addressing regulatory and ethical challenges.

In clinical settings, Generative AI played a pivotal role in decision-making processes. Notable applications included the integration of Generative AI in digital pathology for improved cancer detection, as exemplified by Paige.AI, the first company to receive FDA approval for AI use in this domain. Additionally, AI-driven solutions like Abridge and DeepScribe demonstrated the potential to automate administrative tasks such as documentation and patient onboarding, significantly reducing the workload on healthcare providers.

The pharmaceutical sector benefited immensely from Generative AI, particularly in accelerating drug discovery and precision medicine therapies. A prime example is Insilico Medicine, which leveraged AI to drastically cut down the time and cost involved in developing new drugs. Their work in creating a treatment for idiopathic pulmonary fibrosis is a testament to the efficiency and potential of AI in this field.

However, the integration of AI in healthcare also raised concerns about the accuracy and reliability of AI-generated medical advice. Instances of AI models providing incorrect diagnoses highlighted the importance of verifying AI-generated information in clinical settings. This underscored the necessity for ongoing evaluation and quality assurance in AI applications in healthcare.

Regulatory frameworks began evolving to address the challenges posed by AI. The EU AI Act and the US Executive Order on AI development are examples of legislative efforts to establish guidelines and manage AI risks in healthcare. The US initiative included the formation of an HHS AI Task Force to develop a regulatory action plan for AI-enabled technologies in healthcare.

Looking forward, the potential applications of Generative AI in healthcare are vast. They include real-time patient monitoring, personalized care, and preventive healthcare initiatives. The ongoing development and integration of AI in healthcare promise significant advancements in patient care and the overall efficiency of healthcare systems.

In summary, the exploration of Generative AI in healthcare in 2023 marked a critical step in enhancing clinical practice. While promising, it also highlighted the need for careful consideration of challenges and ethical implications. The continuous evolution and integration of AI in healthcare are poised to bring transformative changes in the near future.

9.12. Generative AI Enhancing Customer Service

The year 2023 marked a significant milestone in the application of Generative AI in customer service sectors. A series of studies and real-world implementations demonstrated how these advanced AI tools, particularly Large Language Models (LLMs), could drastically improve productivity and efficiency in customer-facing roles.

Generative AI tools, equipped with sophisticated natural language processing capabilities, were shown to enhance the quality and speed of customer service. These AI systems could handle a wide range of customer inquiries, from basic questions to more complex issues, with a high degree of accuracy and consistency. For example, Octopus Energy reported an 18% increase in customer happiness scores with AI-drafted emails compared to human-only responses. This capability allowed customer service representatives to focus on more challenging and nuanced customer interactions, thereby increasing overall productivity.

Another key advantage of using Generative AI in customer service was the ability to offer personalized responses to customers. AI tools could analyze customer data and previous interactions to provide tailored responses, enhancing customer satisfaction and engagement. Additionally, these tools were instrumental in automating routine tasks, such as ticket sorting and response drafting, further streamlining the customer service process.

The introduction of AI tools in customer service also had a positive impact on employee experience. By automating repetitive tasks, AI allowed customer service agents to engage in more meaningful and rewarding work. This shift not only improved job satisfaction but also contributed to better employee retention rates.

Despite these benefits, the integration of Generative AI into customer service also presented challenges. Ensuring the accuracy of AI-generated responses and maintaining a balance between automated and human interactions were areas that required careful consideration and adaptation. Training staff to effectively use these tools and addressing potential biases in AI models were also critical for success.

Looking ahead, the studies from 2023 indicated a promising future for Generative AI in customer service. As these tools continue to evolve, they are expected to become even more integral to the customer service industry, offering opportunities for enhanced customer engagement and operational efficiency.

In conclusion, the advancements in Generative AI in 2023 significantly enhanced the capabilities of customer service sectors. By improving productivity, personalization, and employee satisfaction, these AI tools signified a new era in customer service, one that balances technological efficiency with the human touch. The ongoing development of these tools is poised to further revolutionize the way businesses interact with their customers.

9.13. Quantum Computing and 5G Networks Innovations

The year 2023 marked a significant milestone in technological advancements with notable progress in quantum computing and the deployment of 5G networks, both of which had a profound impact on the AI sector.

In quantum computing, 2023 witnessed key advancements, particularly in error correction and diverse technological approaches. Major companies like Google Quantum AI and Quantinuum demonstrated significant progress in assembling qubits into error-correcting ensembles, an essential step towards more reliable quantum computing. IBM's initiatives in reducing error-inducing noise in its machines represented another notable advancement, enhancing computational accuracy. Additionally, various approaches in quantum computing technology, including trapped ion technology by IonQ and Honeywell and photon-based quantum computations by PsiQuantum, indicated a rich exploration within the field, suggesting that a hybrid approach might eventually prevail.

Harvard University's development of the first programmable, logical quantum processor marked a breakthrough in the field. This innovation, based on a neutral atom array system, enables more efficient and scalable control of logical qubits, moving towards practical quantum computing applications.

IBM laid out a comprehensive roadmap for quantum-centric supercomputing, integrating quantum and classical computational elements. This plan, extending to 2033, reflects a long-term commitment to advancing quantum computing towards utility-scale work and a more seamless development environment for users.

In the realm of AI, the capabilities of quantum computing, particularly its ability to operate on qubits that allow for unparalleled parallel processing and efficiency, are set to enhance machine learning and intricate problem-solving. Despite these advancements, challenges such as maintaining qubit stability and scalability persist, requiring ongoing innovation and investment.

Concurrently, the rollout of 5G networks significantly altered the digital infrastructure landscape. Known for its high-speed data transfer and reduced latency, 5G technology facilitated more efficient and real-time data processing. This was especially beneficial for AI applications requiring immediate data analysis and response, such as autonomous vehicles, IoT devices, and smart city implementations.

The synergy between quantum computing's processing capabilities and 5G's high-speed connectivity offered a transformative potential for the AI sector. While quantum computing provided the power to tackle complex AI algorithms, 5G networks ensured seamless, real-time operation of AI systems.

However, alongside these advancements, challenges remained. Quantum computing faced hurdles in stability, error rates, and scalability. Similarly, the widespread implementation of 5G networks required significant infrastructural changes and raised concerns over security and privacy.

Looking forward, the ongoing developments in quantum computing and 5G networks are poised to create a more interconnected and efficient technological ecosystem. Their impact on AI is expected to grow exponentially, leading to more advanced, efficient, and intelligent AI systems.

In conclusion, the innovations in quantum computing and the rollout of 5G networks in 2023 represented major technological advancements with far-reaching implications for the AI sector. These developments not only enhanced the capabilities of AI systems but also provided a glimpse into the future of technology, where speed, efficiency, and intelligence converge to create a more connected and smarter world.

9.14. Conclusion and a Word About Regularization

The year 2023 marked a significant chapter in the evolution of Generative AI, laying a foundation for transformative changes across various sectors. From the advancements in ChatGPT and AI coding assistants to breakthroughs in synthetic media, 3D asset creation, and multimodal AI models, this year has been pivotal in demonstrating the vast potential and impact of AI technologies.

However, it's essential to recognize that 2023 was just the beginning. With the accelerating pace of AI development, we anticipate that the first half of the following year alone will bring more advancements than the entirety of 2023. This rapid progression underscores the importance of ongoing innovation, ethical considerations, and regulatory measures to ensure responsible and beneficial use of AI.

As we move forward, the journey with AI continues to be one of exploration and discovery, promising to reshape our world in ways we are just beginning to comprehend. The future of AI, burgeoning with possibilities, invites us to engage with these technologies thoughtfully and creatively, shaping a future where AI enhances and enriches the human experience.

It's time for a serious conversation about the regulation of Artificial Intelligence, particularly the realm of Generative AI. I firmly believe that a judicious level of regulation is not only sensible but necessary. However, I advocate for a nuanced approach that tailors regulations to specific applications rather than imposing broad, technology-wide constraints. While legislative bodies such as the EU undoubtedly act with the best of intentions, we must be cautious. Overregulation could strangle the very technology we need to evolve as a society—culturally, morally, and technologically. Let us navigate this new frontier with care, ensuring that regulation fosters growth rather than stifles innovation.

9.15. References

- Advanced. *"A Year of Milestones: Unveiling the Transformative Advances in AI in 2023."*
  https://www.oneadvanced.com/news-and-opinion/a-year-of-milestones-unveiling-the-transformative-advances-in-ai-in-2023/

- McKinsey. "*The State of AI in 2023: Generative AI's Breakout Year.*" https://www.mckinsey.com/business-functions/mckinsey-digital/our-insights/the-state-of-ai-in-2023-generative-ais-breakout-year
- MIT Technology Review. "*Four Trends That Changed AI in 2023*" https://www.technologyreview.com/2023/12/19/1085696/four-trends-that-changed-ai-in-2023/
- Stanford University. "*13 Biggest AI Stories 2023.*" https://hai.stanford.edu/news/13-biggest-ai-stories-2023
- Gradient Flow. "*Generative AI 2023: Why This Year Marks a Major Turning Point.*" https://gradientflow.com/generative-ai-2023-why-this-year-marks-a-major-turning-point/
- AI Dailies. "*The Future of Generative AI in 2023.*" https://aidailies.com/the-future-of-generative-ai-in-2023/
- Technology Magazine. "*Top 10 Biggest Innovations 2023.*" https://technologymagazine.com/top10/top-10-biggest-innovations-of-2023
- Deeper Insights. "*ChatGPT Technical Innovations and Business Impacts in 2023.*" https://deeperinsights.com/ai-blog/chatgpt-technical-innovations-and-business-impacts-in-2023
- Nature. "*ChatGPT and science: the AI system was a force in 2023 — for good and bad.*" https://www.nature.com/articles/d41586-023-03930-6
- Search Engine Journal. "*ChatGPT Celebrates Its First Birthday After Notable AI Advances.*" https://www.searchenginejournal.com/chatgpt-a-look-back-at-one-year-of-ai-advances-from-openai/502664/
- TechRepublic. "*ChatGPT 1-Year Anniversary: How Generative AI Has Evolved.*" https://www.techrepublic.com/article/chatgpt-one-year-anniversary-2023-insights/
- MIT Technology Review. "*How AI Assistants are Already Changing the Way Code Gets Made.*" https://www.technologyreview.com/2023/12/06/1084457/ai-assistants-copilot-changing-code-software-development-github-openai/
- BloomDev. "*Top 6 AI Coding Assistants in 2023.*" https://bloomdev.ca/top-6-ai-coding-assistants-in-2023/

- Softkraft. *"Top 3 AI Coding Assistants to Accelerate Software Delivery in 2023."*
  https://www.softkraft.co/ai-coding-assistants/
- Synaptic Labs. *"The Rise of Synthetic Media: A Brave New World or a Dark Path Ahead?"*
  https://blog.synapticlabs.ai/the-rise-of-synthetic-media
- Unite.AI. *"Synthetic Media – Types, Application, & Ethical Ramifications."*
  https://www.unite.ai/synthetic-media-types-application-ethical-ramifications/
- NVIDIA Technical Blog. *"Most Popular NVIDIA Technical Blog Posts 2023: Generative AI, LLMS, Robotics, Virtual Worlds Breakthroughs."*
  https://developer.nvidia.com/blog/year-in-review-trending-posts-of-2023/
- Oracle. *"Generative AI: The Future of Game Asset Creation at GDC 2023."*
  https://blogs.oracle.com/cloud-infrastructure/post/generative-ai-game-asset-creation-gdc-2023
- NVIDIA Blog. *"Latest NVIDIA Graphics Research Advances Generative AI."*
  https://blogs.nvidia.com/blog/graphics-research-advances-generative-ai-next-frontier/
- Garagefarm. *"Adobe's 2023 Innovations: A Boon for 3D Artists."*
  https://garagefarm.net/blog/adobes-2023-innovations-a-boon-for-3d-artists
- Grid Dynamics. *"2023 Trends: Hyper-personalization in Customer-Facing Technologies."*
  https://blog.griddynamics.com/2023-trends-hyper-personalization-in-customer-facing-technologies
- Ortto. *"Emerging Personalization Trends in Marketing 2023."*
  https://ortto.com/learn/personalization-trends-in-2023/
- Microsoft Research. *"Research at Microsoft 2023: A year of Groundbreaking AI Advances and Discoveries."*
  https://www.microsoft.com/en-us/research/blog/research-at-microsoft-2023-a-year-of-groundbreaking-ai-advances-and-discoveries/
- KPMG. *"Generative AI Survey Report."*
  https://advisory-marketing.us.kpmg.com/speed/genai2023.html
- BCG. *"For Global Business Services, Generative AI Creates Four Big Opportunities."*
  https://www.bcg.com/publications/2023/genai-creates-four-key-business-opportunities

- Bain & Company. *"The Talent Implications of Generative AI."* https://www.bain.com/insights/the-talent-implications-of-generative-ai-tech-report-2023/
- Covington & Burling LLP. *"U.S. Artificial Intelligence Policy: Legislative and Regulatory Developments."* https://www.cov.com/en/news-and-insights/insights/2023/10/us-artificial-intelligence-policy-legislative-and-regulatory-developments
- Goodwin. *"US Artificial Intelligence Regulations: Watch List for 2023."* https://www.goodwinlaw.com/en/insights/publications/2023/04/04_12-us-artificial-intelligence-regulations
- Alston & Bird. *"AI Regulation in the U.S.: What's Coming, and What Companies Need to Do in 2023."* https://www.alston.com/en/insights/publications/2022/12/ai-regulation-in-the-us
- Brookings. *"The US Government Should Regulate AI if it Wants to Lead on International AI Governance."* https://www.brookings.edu/articles/the-us-government-should-regulate-ai/
- DLA Piper. *"US senators introduce bill to establish AI governance framework."* https://www.dlapiper.com/en-cl/insights/publications/ai-outlook/2023/us-senators-introduce-bill-to-establish-ai-governance-framework
- Reuters. *"Explainer: What's Next for the EU AI Act?"* https://www.reuters.com/technology/whats-next-eu-ai-act-2023-12-14/
- MIT Technology Review. *"Five Things You Need to Know About the EU's New AI Act."* https://www.technologyreview.com/2023/12/11/1084942/five-things-you-need-to-know-about-the-eus-new-ai-act/
- Arxiv. *"DetectGPT: Zero-Shot Machine-Generated Text Detection using Probability Curvature."* https://arxiv.org/abs/2301.11305
- Arxiv. *"Fast-DetectGPT: Efficient Zero-Shot Detection of Machine-Generated Text via Conditional Probability Curvature."* https://arxiv.org/abs/2310.05130
- Tech Xplore. *"Human or AI Writer? Scholars Develop Tool for Detection."* https://techxplore.com/news/2023-02-human-writer-ai-scholars-tool.html
- Synced Review. *"Stanford DetectGPT Takes a Curvature-Based Approach to LLM-Generated Text Detection."*

https://syncedreview.com/2023/02/01/stanford-detectgpt-takes-a-curvature-based-approach-to-llm-generated-text-detection/

- Gizmodo Australia. *"New 'DetectGPT' Tool Could Bring an End to AI Cheating on Exams"*
https://gizmodo.com.au/2023/01/detectgpt-cheating-ai/

- The Decoder. *"Stanford DetectGPT and GPTZeroX: New tools for AI text recognition."*
https://the-decoder.com/stanford-detectgpt-and-gptzerox-new-tools-for-ai-text-recognition/

- BCG. *"How Generative AI is Transforming Healthcare."*
https://www.bcg.com/publications/2023/how-generative-ai-is-transforming-health-care-sooner-than-expected

- Deloitte. *"Generative AI Holds Enormous Promise for Health Care."*
https://www2.deloitte.com/us/en/blog/health-care-blog/2023/generative-ai-holds-enormous-promise-for-health-care.html

- McKinsey. *"Generative AI in Healthcare: Emerging Use for Care."*
https://www.mckinsey.com/industries/healthcare/our-insights/tackling-healthcares-biggest-burdens-with-generative-ai

- FODH. *"UPSIDE DOWN: How AI Changed Healthcare in 2023."*
https://fodh.substack.com/p/how-ai-changed-healthcare-2023

- BCG. *"How Generative AI Is Already Transforming Customer Service."*
https://www.bcg.com/publications/2023/how-generative-ai-transforms-customer-service

- TechTarget. *"In 2023, Generative AI Made Inroads in Customer Service."*
https://www.techtarget.com/searchcustomerexperience/feature/In-2023-generative-AI-made-inroads-in-customer-service

- Phys.org. *"Quantum Computing Technologies."*
https://phys.org/news/2023-10-quantum-theyre.html

- TechXplore. *"Harvard's Quantum Computing Breakthrough."*
https://techxplore.com/news/2023-12-programmable-logical-quantum-processor.html

- The Quantum Insider. *"A Century in The Making: IBM Quantum's Development Roadmap, Building The Future of a Nascent Technology."*
https://thequantuminsider.com/2022/06/30/a-century-in-the-making-ibm-quantums-development-roadmap-building-the-future-of-a-nascent-technology/

- Analytics Vidhya. *"The Role of Quantum Computing in AI."* https://www.analyticsvidhya.com/blog/2023/12/the-role-of-quantum-computing-in-advancing-artificial-intelligence/

9.16. Prompts

Generative AI brain:
- a central, large, translucent, futuristic brain representing Generative AI.
- Steps: 20
- Sampler: DPM++ 2M Karras
- CFG scale: 7
- Seed: 2335815429
- Size: 1344x768
- Model: albedobaseXL_v13

10. How to become (more of) a Cyborg?

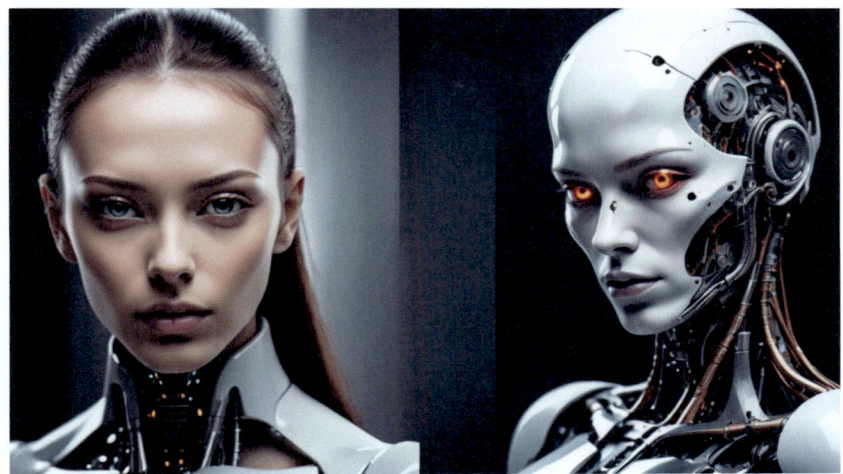

There are good and there are evil cyborgs. While the first are a near-future reality, the latter are and will remain fiction.

Imagine stepping beyond the bounds of your natural abilities, merging the organic with the synthetic to become something more—a cyborg. This isn't the stuff of science fiction nightmares; it's an evolution already in motion. A cyborg, or a cybernetic organism, is a fusion of flesh and technology, a melding of human and machine that transcends our biological limitations.

From the subtle to the sublime, cyborgs exist on a spectrum. They might be as unassuming as someone wearing glasses—yes, even your spectacles are a technological enhancement—or as sophisticated as individuals sporting neural interfaces or robotic limbs. The essence of cyborg existence is about upgrading ourselves, interlacing our human capabilities with the power of technology.

Consider the everyday marvels of modern medicine: pacemakers that keep hearts beating in rhythm, cochlear implants that gift the joy of sound, and insulin pumps that meticulously manage diabetes. Then there's the smartphone, an external brain that stores our memories, manages our schedules, and connects us across continents.

In the pages ahead, we'll dive into the realm of white-collar work and explore how you can embrace your inner cyborg, enhancing your professional prowess and perhaps even redefining what it means to be human. Join us on this extraordinary journey to discover how to intertwine your life with the digital world and unleash the full potential of your cyborg self.

Before I will give you a few hints remember, becoming a cyborg using Generative AI is a unique and evolving field. Stay curious, continuously educate yourself, and remain open to the possibilities offered by this technology. As you explore, adapt, and create, you'll be carving a path towards merging your organic self with generative technologies to become a true cyborg.

10.1. Familiarize yourself with Generative AI

Embarking on the path to becoming a cyborg is not just about the hardware — it's about expanding your mental capabilities. At the heart of this transformation lies Generative AI, a thrilling frontier in technology that empowers machines to create new, never-before-seen data, environments, and life-like entities. To embrace your cyborg potential, you must delve into the world of generative models and deep learning, the bedrock of Generative AI.

These generative models are not just algorithms; they are like digital alchemists, conjuring up fresh data samples from the ether of existing information. Deep learning, a subset of machine learning, unfolds the mysteries of data through layers of artificial neural networks, teaching machines to predict and innovate.

To guide you on this quest, there are countless resources at your disposal. Class Central opens doors to over 2,700 free courses and 1,900 paid courses, giving you the keys to unlock the secrets of tools like ChatGPT, Midjourney, and Stable Diffusion. There, you will find a treasure trove of knowledge on a breadth of Generative AI topics.

Coursera beckons with its vast selection of Generative AI training courses, offering both free and premium options, with the added perk of certificates to showcase your newfound expertise. Standout courses cover exciting subjects such as Generative AI with Large Language Models and the art of Prompt Engineering for ChatGPT.

EdX invites learners of all levels to explore its rich repository of Generative AI resources, featuring courses on prompt engineering, ethical considerations, and real-world applications. Many of these courses even offer a free audit option for the curious mind.

Google Cloud steps in with an Introduction to Generative AI Learning Path, a free course that lays the foundation of generative AI, Large Language

Models, and the principles of responsible AI practice. This course is enriched with live training sessions and hands-on labs.

For those who crave a community experience, Towards AI stands out as a vibrant platform, boasting contributions from over 2,000 writers. It's a place to stay on the pulse of AI, with a plethora of news, opinions, tutorials, and discussions on the latest trends.

Udemy caters to beginners eager to dip their toes into Generative AI waters, offering courses that span from ChatGPT basics to AI's transformative role in marketing and cybersecurity.

Google's Intro to Generative AI courses are a wellspring of knowledge, complete with engaging video instruction, curated reading lists, quizzes, and practical online labs, covering everything from image generation to the ethics of AI.

For those who yearn for a deeper dive, books like "Generative Deep Learning, 2nd Edition" by O'Reilly Media offer a comprehensive exploration of Generative AI's facets, including Conditional GANs, LSTM Networks, and Diffusion Models.

With these resources, learners of all stripes — from AI novices to seasoned machine learning practitioners — can significantly elevate their understanding and skills in the dynamic realm of Generative AI.

Searching for the perfect starting point can be daunting, but let me assure you, the abundance of quality resources available today means you're almost guaranteed to stumble upon something worthwhile. So take the plunge—your journey to knowledge awaits. Start now, and start with confidence!

You can start here:

- TechTarget: Top 10 generative AI courses and training resources
  https://www.techtarget.com
- freeCodeCamp: Intro to Generative AI – 10 Free Courses by Google
  https://www.freecodecamp.org
- O'Reilly Media: Generative Deep Learning, 2nd Edition
  https://www.oreilly.com

10.2. 2. Embrace the Power of ChatGPT

Dive into the world of Generative AI with ChatGPT. Despite my critiques of OpenAI, their creation stands out as a learning powerhouse. Make ChatGPT your go-to companion and integrate it into your daily routine. Ponder the possibilities: Can ChatGPT enhance this? Can it take the lead? Embark on this journey and let ChatGPT illuminate the path to innovation.

As someone who questions the credibility and reliability of technology, ChatGPT is truly remarkable. It's affordable and easily accessible, allowing a wide range of individuals to expand their knowledge and explore their imaginations.

Imagine having a reliable and intelligent companion available to you anytime. ChatGPT makes this dream a reality. Its vast database and neural network capabilities provide a conversational partner who is responsive, thought-provoking, and insightful.

Integrating ChatGPT into your daily routine can be a game-changer. It offers a fresh perspective and knowledge that can elevate your work. Whether you're a writer, student, or professional, ChatGPT has your back.

One fascinating aspect of ChatGPT is its ability to lead conversations. Engage in dynamic exchanges, where ChatGPT challenges your assumptions and expands your understanding.

Examples:

1. Brainstorming ideas: ChatGPT serves as a valuable brainstorming partner, providing fresh perspectives and suggesting new concepts.
2. Learning and research assistance: ChatGPT is a reliable resource for finding information and answering questions, saving you time and effort.
3. Writing and editing support: ChatGPT assists with drafting, gives feedback, and can help improve your writing style.
4. Professional development: ChatGPT acts as a virtual mentor, providing insights and advice for career growth and workplace challenges.

Let's talk about the power of responsibility. You might find yourself placing great trust in the capabilities of ChatGPT, and while that trust is often well-founded, it's wise to maintain a healthy dose of skepticism and critical thinking. Even though ChatGPT can be impressively accurate, it's not infallible. Remember, the final judgment rests with you, and that's not changing anytime soon.

10.3. Engage with the Generative AI community

Embarking on a journey into the world of Generative AI is not only about absorbing information; it's about actively engaging with a vibrant community that shares your passion. Here are some pathways to immerse yourself in this dynamic field:

Firstly, online forums and discussion groups offer a treasure trove of knowledge and interaction. Whether it's Reddit's r/MachineLearning, LinkedIn groups, or Stack Overflow discussions, these platforms provide a space to ask questions, share experiences, and learn from a diverse group of enthusiasts and experts.

Virtual conferences and webinars, hosted by major tech companies and academic institutions, are a goldmine for those looking to dive deep into the latest research and applications in AI. Events like NeurIPS or the O'Reilly AI Conference bring together leading minds in the field, offering invaluable insights and networking opportunities.

For a more hands-on approach, participating in hackathons and AI competitions, such as those on Kaggle, can be both exhilarating and educational. These events challenge you to apply your skills in practical scenarios, fostering learning through doing.

Staying updated with blogs and YouTube channels dedicated to AI is another effective way to keep pace with the rapidly evolving field. These platforms are filled with tutorials, discussions, and news, making learning both accessible and engaging.

Social media groups on platforms like Twitter and LinkedIn, along with relevant hashtags like #GenerativeAI, are buzzing with professionals sharing their insights, research, and the latest industry news. These platforms are perfect for quick updates and networking.

Collaborating on open-source projects is a unique way to contribute to the AI community while enhancing your own skills. GitHub, for instance, is a hub for such collaboration, where you can both learn from others' code and contribute your own.

Enrolling in online courses and workshops often comes with the added benefit of community interaction. These platforms not only provide structured learning but also enable you to connect with fellow learners and instructors, enriching your learning experience.

Lastly, local meetups and user groups offer a more personal setting for networking and learning. Depending on your location, these groups can provide face-to-face interactions, making for a more intimate learning environment.

In conclusion, the journey through the world of Generative AI is made richer and more fulfilling by engaging with its community. By participating actively, asking questions, and sharing your knowledge, you not only enhance your own understanding but also contribute to the growth of this exciting field.

Remember, the key to benefiting from these communities is not just passive consumption of information, but active participation. Ask questions, share your knowledge, and engage with others. This not only enhances your learning experience but also helps you build a network of contacts who share your interest in Generative AI.

10.4. Experiment and create

The journey to becoming a cyborg through Generative AI is an invigorating mix of learning, community interaction, and above all, experimenting and creating. This transformative journey begins with small-scale projects. Whether it's crafting a chatbot or a simple AI program tailored to your passion, these projects are vital for grasping the practical elements of AI like coding, data management, and algorithm refinement.

The next step is to engage with real-world challenges. By participating in or initiating projects that address societal issues in areas like healthcare, education, or environmental conservation, you apply your skills in meaningful ways. Platforms like GitHub are ideal for finding collaboration opportunities.

A significant aspect of this journey is exploring AI's creative potential. You might dive into digital art, music, writing, or other artistic ventures, using tools like DALL-E or GPT-3. This exploration showcases how AI can enhance human creativity.

Another exciting avenue is developing personalized AI tools. Whether it's a bespoke recommendation system, a personal assistant for daily tasks, or a specialized data analysis tool, tailoring AI to meet your specific needs enhances your skillset and adds a personal dimension to your cyborg journey.

Participation in AI challenges and competitions is also crucial. These platforms, found on websites like Kaggle, DrivenData, or AIcrowd, push your creative and technical boundaries by challenging you to solve complex problems under specific constraints.

An integral part of your journey is sharing your creations with the AI community. By documenting and showcasing your work through blogs, videos, or social media, you invite feedback, encourage collaboration, and increase your visibility in the field. This not only acts as a portfolio of your capabilities but also fosters a collaborative spirit.

Importantly, the development process in AI is iterative. Continuously refining your projects based on new learnings, feedback, and technological advancements keeps your work relevant and effective. It's a process that keeps you actively engaged with the ever-evolving landscape of AI.

In conclusion, the path to cyborg transformation through Generative AI is a thrilling blend of education, collaboration, experimentation, and innovation. By starting with manageable projects, tackling real-world problems, unleashing your creativity with AI, and sharing your journey, you actively shape the future of this field. Every small step you take is a significant stride towards realizing your potential as a cybernetic organism.

10.5. Conclusion: Embracing the Cyborg Within

In our exploration of becoming more cyborg through the integration of Generative AI, we've journeyed through a landscape where the lines between human and machine blur, not into a dystopian haze, but into a harmonious symphony of enhanced capabilities and expanded consciousness.

The path to embracing your inner cyborg is a rich tapestry of opportunities, interwoven with technology, creativity, and community. Engaging with AI enthusiasts, participating in discussions, and diving into projects are all part of this journey. It's about continuously evolving, embracing change, and seeing the merging of human and machine as an expansion of humanity rather than a loss.

Your cyborg transformation is an ongoing process, a never-ending adventure into the realms of possibility. It's about harnessing the power of AI to not only enhance your capabilities but also to deepen your understanding of the world and yourself. It's an invitation to be part of something greater, a future where technology and humanity coalesce into something far more profound than their separate parts.

So, as you turn the page, carry with you the lessons learned, the curiosity sparked, and the vision of a future where you, as a cyborg, play a pivotal role in shaping a world where technology amplifies the best of what it means to be human. The journey continues, and the future is not just something to be experienced, but something to be created. Embrace it with open arms and an open mind.

10.6. Prompts

Cyborgs:
- Positive prompt: image of a good and an evil cyborg. split image. futuristic photograph. high tech. masterpiece photography.
- Steps: 20
- Sampler: DPM++ 2M Karras
- CFG scale: 7
- Seed: 223400365
- Size: 1344x768
- Model: albedobaseXL_v13

11. Conclusion

What an exhilarating journey 2023 has been! It was a year that stirred a whirlpool of creative energy, especially within the Generative AI community. This exceptional group of visionaries, spanning various fields of creativity and productivity, demonstrated how Deep Neural Networks can enhance human potential. The benefits, as we've seen, substantially outweigh the minimal risks. If you're reading this, chances are, you're already a member of this unique, global cyberpunk family. If not, consider this your warm invitation!

Unexpectedly, Artificial Intelligence has become a primary driver of human innovation and progress—something I had envisioned happening much later in my lifetime. The developments we've seen unfold in 2023 were beyond anyone's predictions, yet they've swiftly become integral to our daily existence.

The year 2023 marked a significant personal transformation for me too. As an artist in residence, I embraced the notion of becoming more cyborg-like. Through this book, I extend an invitation to you to discover your own inner cyborg. Fear not! Unlike dystopian video games or Hollywood movies, this transformation is a positive and painless process. Enjoy the journey!

This book has chronicled my creative journey throughout 2023. I am deeply grateful that you chose to accompany me on this exploration. Writing this has allowed me to gain perspective and I eagerly anticipate the future of Generative Artificial Intelligence. Here's to the promising years ahead!

Thanks for reading and never hesitate to reach out to me!

12. Acknowledgements

Expressing humble gratitude to all those people who inspired this work.

Having penned the final chapter of this book a moment ago, I am compelled to extend my heartfelt thanks to the myriad individuals, collectives, and institutions that have energized this year. The vibrancy of 2023 has been remarkable, and it's clear that the events and developments of this year would have taken a different shape—or perhaps not occurred at all—without the contributions of those I am about to acknowledge.

KI Salon Heilbronn, especially Thomas Bornheim, Lea Krück, and Robert Mucha, for providing the fertile soil to my creativity to grow on, and the KI Salon community for their constant and unwavering support. Thanks to Peter

Hahn, Marcel Fortuin, Rolf Petermann - van den Berg, Dieter Herzig, Jochen Stein, Jens Ewald and all the others.

Bruno Kramm for his constant inspiration and support and for always showing that the computer is one of the most powerful musical instruments.

Dieter Schwarz and the Dieter Schwarz Stiftung for so generously funding the art residency.

STACKIT GmbH from Neckarsulm, especially Bastian Tiefenbach, Marvin Titus, Christian Harms, and Yannic Rubenzer, for providing GPU compute and their constant help and guidance.

MIFCOM GmbH from Munich, especially Michael Bucher and Wolfram Hausmann, for their fantastic support with my own AI workstation and the one we bought for KI Salon Heilbronn.

The "gang" from Hamburg, especially Britta Leusing from KI Campus, plus Werner Bogula and Alois Krtil from ARIC, for a lot of fun and insights, and the creative connection to the North.

KI Bundesverband for their support and the great work they are doing for Germany and Europe, especially Jörg Bienert and Vanessa Cann.

42 Heilbronn for doing the great work and facilitating next generation digital education, and also for supporting my endeavors with space, inspiration, help and sparkling water on tap. Thanks especially to Pascal Rüger, Markus Hagner, Debbie Gunkel, Moritz Carthaus, Nadia Aleksan, Steve Killian and Ines Rose.

Sven Körner for showing that Computer Science and music have a huge overlap. Bringing my AI to the stage will never be forgotten.

Data Science Retreat for forgiving me that I did not have enough time to mentor their students this year and for allowing me to inspire their students with Generative AI.

Sabine "bleeptrack" Wieluch for all the nice discussions and for showing the world the beauty of computational creativity.

Patrick Glauner for educating the public and the public servants about Artificial Intelligence.

AlephAlpha, especially Jonas Andrulis and Lorenz Lehmhaus, for their strong vision and mission to unfold the creative and productive potential of Generative AI in Germany.

Ipai, especially Moritz Gräter and Constanze Zawadzky, for showing that AI without culture is like a heart with a weak heartbeat.

And finally thanks to my lovely and beloved wife Dominika Heublein-Behrens for always being at and almost always being on my side. Without her, a lot of things would not have been possible. This book would not look so great, if it was not for her creativity and craftmanship.

I might have forgotten a few. If so, it was not on purpose. Thanks!

12.1. Prompts

Thankfulness:
- Positive prompt: symmetric portrait of a cybernetic human bowing in thankfulness with green glowing eyes and a grateful smile with his hands folded in prayer in front of his chest. he wears glasses and has a beard and wears a black hoodie.
- Negative prompt: dark eyes, brown eyes, out of frame, lowres, text, error, cropped, worst quality, low quality, jpeg artifacts, ugly, duplicate, morbid, mutilated, out of frame and , extra fingers, mutated hands, poorly drawn hands, poorly drawn face, mutation, deformed, blurry, dehy drated, bad anatomy, bad proportions, extra limbs, cloned face, disfigured, gross proportions, malformed limbs, missing arms, missing legs, extra arms, extra legs, fused fingers, too many fingers, long neck, username, watermark, signature
- Steps: 20
- Sampler: DPM++ 2M Karras
- CFG scale: 7
- Seed: 829785871
- Size: 1024x1024
- Model: albedobaseXL_v13